The Ar

D0561919

The Arts Go To School
An Arts-In-Education Handbook

New England Foundation for the Arts

American Council for the Arts

First Edition: 1983

This book is published by:

New England Foundation for the Arts
25 Mount Auburn Street, Cambridge, Massachusetts 02138

American Council for the Arts
570 Seventh Avenue, New York, New York 10018

NX
303
· A76
1983

Library of Congress Cataloging in Publication Data

Main entry under title:

The Arts go to school.

    Bibliography: p.
    Includes index.
    1. Arts—Study and teaching—United States. 2. Artists
as teachers—United States. I. American Council for the
Arts. II. New England Foundation for the Arts.

NX303.A76   1983   700'.7'1073   83-11850
ISBN 0-915400-44-8

Additional copies may be obtained from:

American Council for the Arts
570 Seventh Avenue
New York, New York 10018
212-354-6655

The Arts Go To School

Funds for the original publication of this book were provided by:

> Chesebrough-Pond's Inc.
> Digital Equipment Corporation
> National Endowment for the Arts
> Raytheon Company
> and
> David Rockefeller, Jr.

Project Director:	Thomas Wolf, Executive Director New England Foundation for the Arts
Principal Authors:	Sharon Hya Grollman, Research Assistant Harvard University Project Zero
	Polly Price, Executive Director Cultural Education Collaborative
	Dennie P. Wolf, Research Associate Harvard University Project Zero
	Thomas Wolf, Executive Director New England Foundation for the Arts
Development Team:	Barbara Abendschein, Artists in Schools Coordinator New Hampshire Commission on the Arts
	Kissette Bundy, Coordinator for Artists Programs Massachusetts Council on the Arts and Humanities
	Alan Davis, Artists In Residence Coordinator Vermont Council on the Arts
	Stuart Kestenbaum, Artists in Residence Associate Maine State Commission on the Arts and Humanities
	Jane Mahoney, Director of Education Programs Rhode Island State Council on the Arts
	Jo-Anna Moore, Maine Arts Education Projects University of Southern Maine
Editor:	Cynthia Hartnett
Book Design:	The Laughing Bear Associates

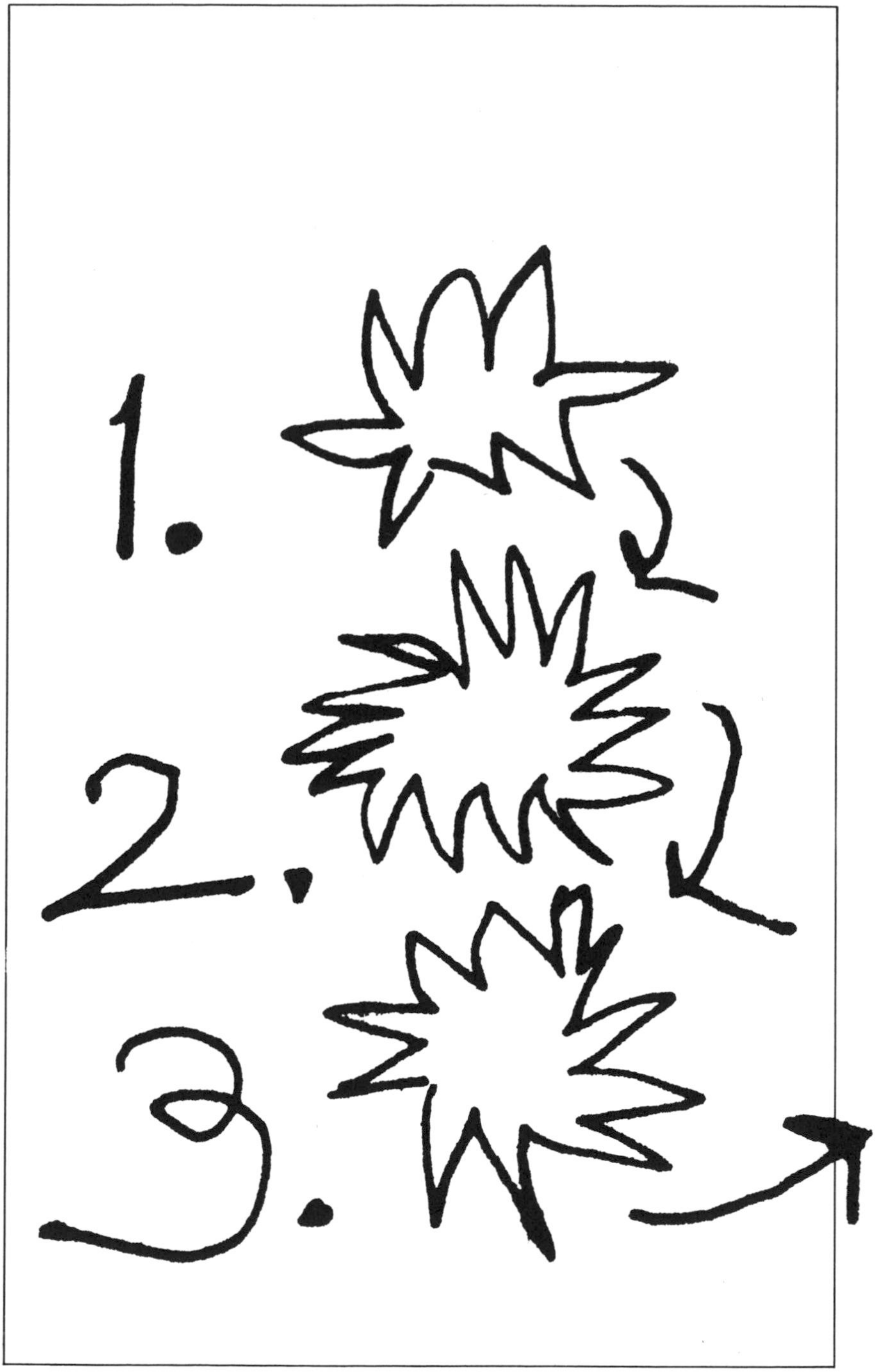
1.
2.
3.

Contents

Introduction

The Thoroughfare Elementary School sits at the top of a hill on North Haven Island in Maine, eleven miles from the mainland. In 1968, it had 48 pupils, ranging in age from four to thirteen, in two rooms. Its teachers that year were my wife, Dennie, and myself. We were just out of college. We had never taught school before and there we were, expected to teach everything from reading, writing, arithmetic, social studies, and science to art, music, and gym. There was a music teacher that came by boat once a week when the weather was good and once or twice a year, there would be a visit from a professional performing group or a visual artist. These visits were particularly special to us and to the kids. They made the art and music come alive in a way that we could not. They gave us something to build upon; they generated excitement; they made the arts into something concrete and the artists into real people.

Some years later I started playing school concerts and doing educational residencies as a flutist with a chamber music group. My perspective had changed and it became more difficult to recall my days as a teacher. I often got discouraged and can remember on one occasion, as I carried a colleague's harp from her stationwagon through the snow and then upstairs to a jam-packed assembly room, wondering privately to myself whether the effort was really worth it. But then during the second year of our residencies, something happened that convinced me just how valuable our visits were. A second-grade teacher came up to me after a concert with a sheepish grin on her face: "I have a confession to make," she said. "Last year when you were here, I taped your concert and I hope you will let me do it again. It has been tremendously helpful in my work with kids who have reading problems. Many have difficulty with listening skills and the tape is a wonderful teaching tool. Listening to 'Tom's tape' is a special treat for the kids and they are so looking forward to today's concert and a new tape."

This experience brought home to me once again the variety of ways in which arts programs can enrich a child's education. And this conviction about the value of the arts in education has been reinforced many times since, especially now that I have children of my own.

There are many teachers, parents, school administrators, artists, and psychologists who are convinced of the importance of the arts in education. Even so, school arts programs have become increasingly vulnerable in recent years. With scarce resources and tight budgets, many school systems have seen arts programs as expendable "extras" — nice to have in the curriculum when times are good, but simply too expensive when times are tough. Arts advocates have found cost-cutting arguments difficult to counter, the practical importance of the arts difficult to demonstrate, and arguments in favor of the arts in education more subtle than those in favor of reading or mathematics. Many arts supporters have felt further frustrated by not knowing how they could assist in bringing arts programs into the schools. "What can we do," is a refrain heard more and more often, especially from parents who are concerned that the quality and richness of their children's education will be significantly augmented by meaningful exposure and involvement in the arts.

This book has been written for people who believe in the importance of the arts in education and *want to do something about it*. It is a book of practical suggestions. It describes everything from convincing the school board to include a budget line item for arts programs to hiring the artists who will do those programs. It describes program planning, promotion, fund raising, and a host of other details. It suggests how artists and teachers can develop a close working relationship and it describes an appropriate role for parents, school administrators, and others who can be of assistance. Finally, this book points the reader to other publications and service organizations that can be of help.

Two things needed to be stated at the outset. Strong school arts programs should have at their center teaching professionals who are permanently associated with a school or school system. Outside artists and performers can support and enrich a school arts program but they cannot replace art and music teachers who give young people ongoing exposure and training in the arts. It should also be pointed out that there exists today a network of agencies that have been critical in supporting the arts-in-education movement and can be of great assistance to those wishing to develop programs in the schools. State arts agencies, with the assistance and encouragement of the National Endowment for the Arts, have provided both money and expertise to the increasing number of schools that have embarked on artist residencies, performances, lecture demonstrations, and other kinds of educational activities. It was experts from the six New England state arts agencies who provided much of the material for this book, based on their daily experiences with artists and with schools.

Finally, I would like to thank several people who helped make this book possible. Joe Prince, Director of the Artists-in-Education Program of the National Endowment for the Arts, provided early encouragement and funding for the project and commented on an early draft. The Executive Directors of the six New England state arts agencies at the time this book was written offered encouragement and staff assistance in the development of the manuscript: John Coe (New Hampshire), Anne Hawley (Massachusetts), Ellen McCulloch-Lovell (Vermont), Christina White (Rhode Island), Alden Wilson (Maine), Gary Young (Connecticut). Jill Bogard of The Arts, Education and Americans, Inc. provided assistance in the development of the bibliography. Lynn Stephen wrote certain sections of an early draft of Chapter 2. And the very wonderful children's poems and illustrations were done by Rachel Auspitz, Brian Burgess, Owen Bush, Chris Herring, Geoffrey Haun, Daniel Kelley, Clyde Kruskal, Mira Levinson, Joshua Moss, Joshua Nove, Jamal Pearson, Matthew Sills, Ari Vais, Alexis Wolf, and Lea Wolf.

Thomas Wolf
January, 1983

The Arts Go To School
An Arts-In-Education Handbook

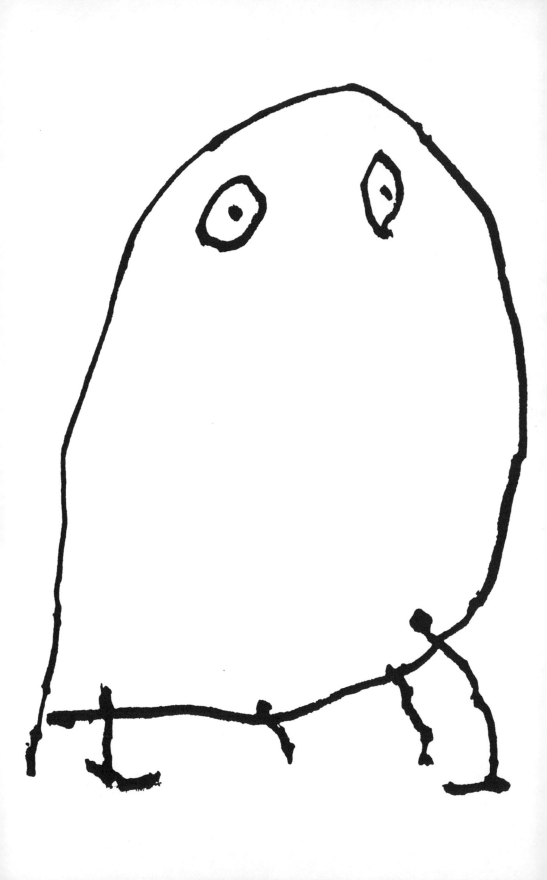

Chapter 1
The Why of Arts in Education

by Dennie Palmer Wolf

One day, between mouthfuls of pizza, your son or daughter grumbles, "There is some dancer coming and it's gonna take up most of our basketball practice. If you think that I'm gonna go out there on my tippy-toes and make a fool of myself, you gotta be crazy." That might be the first and last time that you think about dancers on the basketball court. However, you could also find yourself thinking, "Dancers...I wish they had shown up in my gym class!" or "I'll bet showing them the tremendous physical skill needed for dancing is one great way to cure them of thinking that dancing is for sissies." or "I wish dancers had been a part of the school I went to." If you have thoughts like these, chances are that sooner or later you will find yourself talking about the arts in education with other parents, teachers, and maybe even children.

As you talk, you will inevitably discover that you and others have all kinds of questions about the place of artistic experience in children's education. The more convinced and active you become as an advocate for the arts in education, the more often you will find yourself being asked, "Shouldn't the arts come *after* you have things like reading and math well taken care of?" "Kids can draw in their free time and we have a band, isn't that enough?" "You can only ask schools to do so much, isn't it really up to parents to take their kids to museums and concerts if the arts matter that much to them?" "Young kids are really too little to appreciate art — isn't college the right time for that kind of thing?"

These are tough questions, which are especially hard to answer if you have not been thinking about the issues for long. To help you respond to them, you could turn to materials that argue for the importance of the arts in education. Unfortunately, many of the materials that are ready-to-hand are very general: chapters on the arts in philosophy-of-education books, goal statements from the state department of education, quotes from famous artists describing the importance of the arts in their personal lives. What you find is often inspiring and full of flourish. However, such materials are rarely detailed enough to answer your pressing questions, and they are certainly not specific enough to turn around the thinking of parents, teachers, principals, or superintendents who believe the arts are little more than frosting on basic education. What you need is a short, powerful list of reasons why education is incomplete when it stops short of including the arts.

Have you ever found yourself wishing for a list of reasons for including the arts in education? Have you ever needed to convince your daughter or son, a classroom teacher, a principal, a parent-teacher meeting, or a local business about the importance of the arts but found yourself fumbling around for explanations? If so, then this chapter could be helpful. It brings together a number of concrete arguments for including arts experiences in schooling. For each of these different arguments, this chapter presents examples as well as references to programs and research. While there are many reasons for including the arts as a vital part of any curriculum, this chapter concentrates on three particular families of reasons:

1. Developing imagination and aesthetic understanding.
2. Bolstering the basics.
3. Building community life.

1. WHAT'S SO SPECIAL ABOUT AESTHETIC UNDERSTANDING?

One major part of the business of schools is to teach skills like reading, mathematics, history, and geography, so it is no surprise that classroom walls are covered with reading charts, maps, and chemistry diagrams rather than paintings and rehearsal schedules. In order to make a place for the arts in schools, parents, teachers, and artists often try to dress up the arts in basic skill clothing. In the last ten years, the arts have been advertised like educational aspirin: the best cure-all for ailing classrooms, guaranteed to fix anything from sagging attendence to low reading scores. In the midst of all these promises, we have lost hold of what may be the most fundamental reason for putting artists and children together: when children spend time dancing, making music, or writing poetry, they learn skills and forms of awareness that occur only in the arts. They learn about the "life of the imagination," how to be keen observers and appreciators of experience, how to take pleasure in their own cultural heritage. But saying that will not win you interest, much less support, volunteers, or dollars. You are going to have to be able to say *exactly* why growing up imaginatively and aesthetically matters just like growing up intellectually, physically, or socially matters.

Imagination Counts

What do jazz, copier machines, modern dance, and solar panels have in common? Behind each one of them are inventive, imaginative people who were not satisfied with things being the same old way. Many people think of the arts as a million miles away from anything as practical as a better mousetrap or as serious as science. But, in fact, the arts, just like good science or practical problem solving, require tremendously flexible thinking. It is no accident that one of the greatest painters ever, Leonardo da Vinci, was also an avid scientist and inventor. [1]

In many cases, art-making involves children in experiments and taking risks, leading them out of their "ho-hum" approaches to things and experiences. Take what happened to Miguel, aged 5, when he first began to work with watercolors:

What was going to be a familiar line of blue sky at the top suddenly began to spread and drip, forcing Miguel to invent. What might have been a

standard landscape became "a water world." This sort of invention occurs often in art-making, not just when accidents occur. And the inventing does not stop once children know the tricks of handling paint, clay, and words. In fact, if they have the chance to observe artists and their works, children learn that the arts are *the* place to "go beyond the usual." The two drawings made by the same nine-year-old illustrate this point. The one on the top was made for use in everyday circumstances; it was a sign to go above a cage of chicks in a classroom. The drawing on bottom came out of an art class in which the students imagined and drew fantastic creatures.

Even when children aren't the makers, artworks are great for stirring up curiosity and igniting an interest in invention. A painter can make lines and shapes appear to jump off the page, a mime can walk away without going anywhere, the sounds coming out of instruments can make children feel like laughing or flying. Because artists are interested in stretching old rules and inventing new ones, the things they create are often puzzling — Why would you want to write music for typewriters or radios? How can a sad story be good? Do all dances have to look like Swan Lake? Spending time with artists and artworks isn't the only way to open up to inventiveness or to start asking questions. Good biology or history classes also invite invention and questioning. We teach children to use language in every possible way: through reading *and* writing *and* spelling. Imagination is an equally fundamental skill. We should also teach it with all our available tools: science experiments, investigations in history class, theatre, paintings, music, and dances that ask questions and show new possibilities.

Being Wide Awake to Experience Matters

Imagine that you are awakened by the sound of rain beating on the window near your bed. You can listen to its sound, straining for some clue about whether the window is leaking. You can also hear those same sounds as the raw materials for a musical composition. When you listen as a worried house-owner, you are listening in a very practical way for just one reason. When you listen as a composer might, you get caught up in "thick listening." Everything about the rain becomes interesting: the muffled, liquid sound, the rhythm of the drumming, the surprising little silences. Time spent with the arts can teach just this sort of rich and lively awareness. [2]

This enhanced kind of noticing is so subtle, it is easy to doubt that children are old enough to care about it. But here is a six-year-old talking about what he would like to notice:

If I had three ears, I would listen to the sun
burn, and I would listen to the dragon breathing fire. I would listen to the space ship,
and I would listen to the snake hiss.

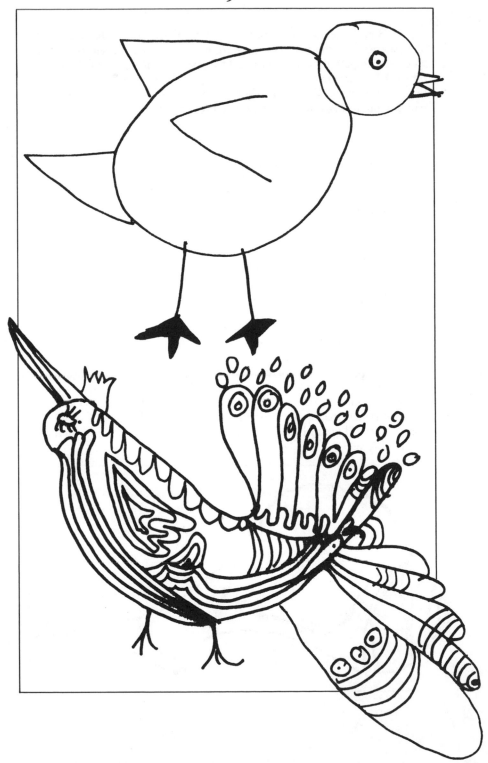

How do we know that spending time with the arts will teach this kind of awareness to children? In answering this question, examples speak loudest. Compare these two versions of a poem about a pack of dogs going off for a run together. One was written by a nine-year-old before he spent time with a writer. The same boy wrote the second poem after the writer sent him out to watch real live dogs parading on a street corner.

POEM #1

There once was a very little dog.
Who had four little legs like little logs.
There once was a big tall dog.
When he ran his long legs went clickety-clog clickety-clog.

POEM #2

The first dog with his four feet
Comes doodling down the alley-way.
The second dog came dippling down that alley-way,
Swirling his eyes round and round.
The third and dizziest, dippling dog
Came slipping down the alley way,
Trying to touch his tail with his tongue.

The process of making art does not simply alert children to the way that words sound or the way clay feels. It can make them sit up and take notice of details that would otherwise escape them. Have a look at all that one ten-year-old noticed about a shell when drawing class turned him into a careful observer.

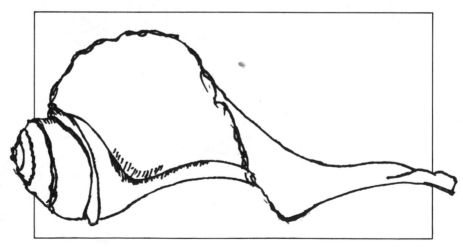

This wide-awake, observant attitude is not limited to noticing how the visual and auditory world appears. The arts can also wake us up to the social world: to other people, to the texture of their lives, to their ideas and feelings. In reading fiction and poetry, children meet up with circumstances very different from their own. Imagine what a city child could learn about country life from reading Robert Frost or what it is possible to learn about growing up black by reading from Gordon Parks, Maya Angelou, or Toni Morrison. Given the power of good writing, children pick up far more than facts from stories and plays. They also are awakened to thinking about friendship, right and wrong, getting old, or what another person's life is like.

The opportunity to "put yourself in someone else's shoes" is especially strong in theatre and mime experiences, where children have to adopt not just the costume but the situation and point of view of another person. In the part of New England once full of mills, a playwright, Carol Korty, mounted a play about the role of child laborers in the strikes at the turn of the century. At various points in the play, teen-age workers talk about being torn between providing for their own well-being and realizing that child laborers take jobs from older workers.

Learning to play such a role wakes children up to the very human experiences of making choices, being afraid, and wrestling with problems. Being in the thick of a dramatic situation makes issues come alive in ways that are simply not available in history book accounts of the mill strikes. If children are going to grow up to be thoughtful, caring adults, this is one form of awareness that is worth transmitting. [3]

Art Works Are Worth Understanding

There is no question in anybody's mind about the importance of literacy. A child who cannot read or write letters and numbers is crippled. Fewer people, however, worry about children's artistic literacy. But what do children lose if they cannot "read" poems, drawings, films, or sculptures?

There is a caricature of the arts as weird activities that no normal person needs to get tangled up with. But the arts are a kind of cultural textbook. There are many times in everyday life when we depend on understanding artistic ideas or processes. All speaking and writing uses language in ways straight out of the arts. [4] Advertisements and political speeches are as full of comparisons and exaggerations as any poem:

"Beer as fresh as a mountain stream"

"My opponent's arguments are mushy."

When people try to express new or complicated ideas, figurative language often provides a way to capture insights: for example, scientists talk about "the milky way" and molecules "bonding." Since stories, poems, and plays depend upon rich language use, they provide an excellent "text" for teaching children to use words fully and flexibly.

Out of the arts also come a host of ideas, images, and characters that are the currency of sharing reactions and impressions. Someone who does not "get" references to princesses, Huck Finn, or Romeo may be locked out of this kind of sharing that goes in novels, jokes, movies.

Aesthetic literacy means understanding "how artworks work." Practically any child can tell you what an astronaut, a space capsule, or radar is. That is pretty amazing, since they have probably never seen any of them except in photographs. By comparison, when a group of researchers asked children what they knew about artworks, children were often mystified or confused. For example, some children thought that paintings were made with cameras and that music was produced by machines.[5] Someone might say, "So what difference does it make if a ten-year-old does not know that music is made by people who are fascinated by what sounds can communicate?" It can make a great deal of difference.

If it is done well, learning about music, dance, or painting includes much more than finding out the definitions of funny new words like "syncopation," "pas de deux," or "tempera." It means learning that artists do not just wake up inspired — they wrestle with ideas, figure out how to capture these ideas in clay, in motion, or in sound, make choices, and take risks. Considered in this way, learning how art and artists work is not so very different from learning to appreciate basketball: If you know what it is like to race up and down the court and try to sink the ball, when a player scores 50 points, your heart is in your throat. Once you know what it is like to try to paint water before a storm or a hot summer sky, Japanese landscape paintings almost take your breath away. If children learn to appreciate the ideas, experiments, and messages in works of art, they have one more source for understanding that human beings are capable of being extra-ordinary.

Many people believe that aesthetic understanding is simply a matter of exposure (your uncle passes along his love of opera by sharing his old record collection) or talent (some people are just born with perfect pitch, bodies good for dancing, lovely voices). In either case, they conclude that it is unnecessary to teach the arts. If you want your schools to offer long-term, serious artistic experiences to children, you are going to have to address questions about whether the arts should belong just to those children who happen to have either "exposure" to the arts or "talent."

Some children come from backgrounds where they learn a great deal about reading before entering kindergarten. Some children also come to school bi-lingual. But in the case of both reading and foreign languages, educators and parents alike argue that these skills are important enough that schools should act to make them available to all children, independent of what they have been or will be exposed to. The arts are no different. Children whose mothers are dancers, whose fathers play in an orchestra, or who are taken to concerts or museums do learn a great deal about art long before adulthood.[6] But if artistic understanding is a part of being human, it should be made available to all children. If schools withhold those experiences, they reinforce the differences in children's backgrounds and reinforce the patterns of advantage.[7]

Talent can provide a critical foundation for aesthetic growth, but even the talented go to teachers, practice, listen to criticism in order to know what to do with their gifts. Moreover, "ordinary" children can learn a great deal about making and enjoying paintings, plays, poems, or dances — if they are given instruction. For example, most children look at paintings as illustrations, noticing only whether the painting is "of" a dog or a boat or a carnival. However, paintings are interesting for their mood, style, and design, as well. But to appreciate these things takes breaking out of old habits and learning to look in new ways. Since many people are never challenged to think about paintings in these new ways, most adults have a hard time with paintings that are not clearly recognizable pictures. However, if children are offered the time and the tools, they begin to look in these novel ways as early as ten or twelve.[8]

2. Aesthetics Are Nice, But What About the Basics?

If you stood up in a parents' meeting and proposed that funds and time be turned over to a program of concerts and exhibits, a forest of hands would shoot up the moment you sat down. Inevitably, a voice would call out, "Imagination is nice, but what about the basics? After all, what good is imagination if you can't write down what you're imagining?" You have to have a strong answer and have it quickly. But what can you say?

First, you have to counter the notion that having a lively arts program will compete with or subtract from the school's concern with basic skills. Do not get bogged down in nit-picking disagreements about whether an arts program would fit neatly into the times set aside for school assemblies. If you can convince your listeners that the arts can invigorate and supplement the teaching of basic skills, the haggling over minutes and spaces can come later. The following are some suggestions for sparking a belief that the arts can bolster basic skills learning:

Art Has More in Common With Reading, Writing, and Arithmetic Than You Think

Past the second month of kindergarten, most basic-skills learning absolutely depends on the ability to handle letters and numbers fluently. Learning to use these and other symbols (like maps and equations) is possibly the biggest task any school-age child faces. Symbol-using skills are just as essential in the arts. Knowing what words to use in what order is as important in writing science fiction stories as it is in writing lab reports. Getting the numbers right matters just as much in musical composition as it does in word problems.

The arts do not offer more "practice and drill" in symbol use; instead they offer children some unique opportunities to figure out how symbols work. In many classrooms, children use "ready-made" symbols like "THE" or "2 + 2" to perform assigned tasks like reading a geography lesson or practicing long division. While there is no doubt about the importance of reading and arithmetic skills, participating in the arts often puts children in the position of inventing their own symbols.[9] Consider what happened when a nine-year-old decided that he wanted to write down a tune he composed. Since he didn't know "the right way" to write music, he had to figure out how to save his composition with symbols of his own making.

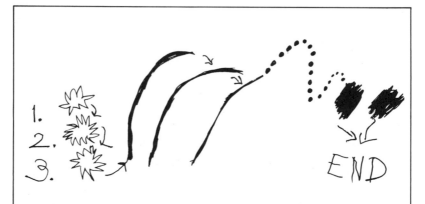

"See here is where the music is supposed to go in three sharp bangs, maybe like car horns; no, like crashes. Over here where the lines get longer, it's for the slower parts that come after. Where all the dots are is for the part when you go up and down the scale: up, down, up. The black patches is when you make this thundering noise in both hands."

Experience with artistic symbol use often provides important, if unrecognized, support to basic symbolic learning. For example, children who have been read to approach the tasks of reading and writing already primed for those tasks. They appear to have a more thorough and complex understanding of grammar. Their familiarity with the way that riddles, rhymes, and stories "go" provides them with a set of expectations that are very helpful. When children meet the word "once," it can be very hard to sound out phonetically. However, if they know that many stories begin with the standard phrase "Once upon a time...," they can often make an "educated" guess and move on to the rest of the sentence. [10]

Even after children learn the conventional ways to write, draw, or record information, the arts continue to provoke experiments with symbols. This is because the idea of finding new, exact, and expressive ways of hearing, seeing and thinking are central to the arts. An eleven-year-old shows this sort of experimental spirit in her search for just the right words to catch what it is like to be zapped by an electric fence:

ELECTRIC FENCES

It zapped through her
And she stood there jimmering
her skin just as live as the skittering crickets.

Three Cheers For Good Old-fashioned "Stick-to-it-ness"

Artists are sometimes characterized as wild-eyed, emotional, fly-by-night creatures. Going along with that caricature is the notion that artworks are born in a flash of inspiration and completed in a wild frenzy. But if you listen to artists, you get quite a different picture. The famous composer Ravel once quipped that "inspiration is the reward for daily work." The poet W.B. Yeats compared writing poems to scrubbing and polishing. Before he completed his famous painting *Guernica*, Picasso went through hundreds of studies and preliminary drawings. So, contrary to the caricature, working with artists may offer children excellent training in a second set of absolutely basic skills: planning, drafting, editing, and polishing. [11]

Many art forms require artists to learn intricate processes. As an artist teaches children to master the steps and techniques in artistic processes, children learn to plan, foresee, and pay close attention. For example, when one sculptor spent time in an industrial arts class, he moved students from the simple processes of cutting and welding by teaching them the ancient and complex technique for casting metals called "the lost wax method." Students, who only weeks earlier had been interested only in welding belt buckles, learned to sculpture wax models of pieces, submerge them in plaster, melt out the wax, pour bronze into the remaining cavity, and then release their work from the plaster. The forethought involved in metal-casting shows up in any number of art forms: the outlines for story plots, drafts of poems, samples of weaving, glaze tests for pottery.

Just as Yeats claims, the arts are full of lessons about the final scrubbing and polishing required before a finished work emerges. Art invites children to invest their own feelings and ideas in their work. As a result, children often stick with their drawings and dances until the last detail is just the way they want it.

Polishing art work involves making personal choices and decisions. It teaches children about judging and using the suggestions or criticisms that come from inside their own heads and from other people. On the facing page is a sequence of drafts for a story that a young writer developed, using both her own ideas and the comments of a writer visiting her class.

Artwork Isn't at Odds With School Work

Art, like gym, is often looked on as a great way for kids to work off extra energy and stray feelings before getting back to "real work." But artwork has a great deal in common with school work. In film-making, as in biology and psychology, people are interested in finding out how the human eye and brain make sense of what is seen. Whether they come out of the seventeenth century or Twyla Tharp's studio, dances often comment on the making and breaking of human relationships. Writers use novels, plays, and poems to analyze what they observe. Think about all that Mark Twain was able to say about the rural South in *Huckleberry Finn*.

In fact, the arts can effectively underscore, illustrate, and even amplify much of what schools want children to learn. What better way to drive home the differences between medieval and modern culture than by comparing court dances with the "bunny hop," "jitterbug," or "disco"? Chamber musicians playing wind or stringed instruments can vividly demonstrate the physics of sound to even young children. A walking tour with an architect can teach children to see and think about the layers of history hidden in the buildings of their own neighborhoods.

Outside of teaching specific content, the arts seem to have a ripple effect on children's level of investment, participation, and curiosity even outside of art class. Far from distracting from basic-skills learning, the arts have been found to stimulate and strengthen it. Elwyn Richardson documents this in his study of the effects of clay work and mask making on a rural classroom. [12] Brooklyn School District 17 ferried over a hundred school children back and forth to the Egyptian collection at the Brooklyn Museum because teachers were certain that the power and mystery of the Egyptian objects would provoke no end of language growth and knowledge change. [13] A recent report on British education summarizes the kind of "lift-off" artwork can provide:

> There is absolutely no sign that an increased attention to the arts...in any way inhibits development of sound basic skills. Very much the reverse seems to be true. The survey found that basic skills were highest where the curriculum was widest...If the basic skills are embedded in a web of direct experience on the part of the child that engages many facets of his (sic) personality and being, then the basic skills grow most strongly. [14]

A.

*Too general
Needs detail*

We had sat here on this bed, when we were smaller, playing at actresses, princesses and important ambassadors.

"Princess Regal?"

"Yes, Sir Ambassador Sebastian?"

"Our enemies seem to be closing in."

*Food, in here
you get real
lively flavor*

"Oh, woe!"

"Owo?"

"No! 'Oh', space, 'woe'. Get it?"

"No... Actually, what I'm really here is to ask you about getting married."

*Too general again
Who's 'people'?*

"Owo." Then we cracked up laughing at how stupid people could be.

B.

It was the same quilted bedspread that we had used for a throne when we played at actresses, princesses and ambassadors.

"Princess Regal?"

"Yes, Sir Ambassador Sebastian?"

"Our enemies seem to be closing in."

"Oh, woe!"

"Owo?"

"No! 'Oh', space, 'woe'. Get it?"

"No... But what I really want, deeply, truly, really is your hand in marriage."

"Owo."

Then we cracked up laughing.

"No, lovely."

"Owo"

"No, deeply."

"Owo."

Then we were laughing too much to talk even.

3. THE ART OF BEING A COMMUNITY

Your pitch about the significance of the arts is only half as strong as it could be if you stop with what arts exposure does for *individual* children. Virtually anyone who has ever had a successful artist residency, performance series, or exhibit wants to talk about the unexpected benefits — about the mural in the front hall, what teachers learned about writing, how older children made scenery for younger students' plays. [15]

Want to Do Away With Some Stereotypes?

When a poet or a photographer becomes a part of a school's routine, all kinds of small changes take place: Students do not always go to the same place at the same time, they are asked to think about new ideas, they often end up working with someone who is not "in their group." Such changes can reorganize people's perceptions of one another. A painter teaching drawing in a vocational arts class learned press printing from students thirty years younger than she! At the end of the painter's residency, an exhibit of drawings in the front hall of the high school made teachers and students from the academic classes "think twice about believing that kids in 'voc ed' don't know which end of the pencil to sharpen." During the first dance residency in a small rural community, a dancer and a drummer worked teaching African folk dances to children. The two of them also worked secretly with teachers. On the last day of the residency, the students got up and performed their dances. Just as they thought the assembly was over, the teachers surprised the children with a performance of their own. The students gave the teachers such a loud and long ovation that the teachers performed an encore. Following the assembly the principal said, "I've been in teaching for eleven years and I've never seen students respond to their teachers like that."

Every school is a collection of different groups — the academic and the vocational students, the Spanish and the English speakers, the brighter, the average, and the special education students. Many schools have found that the arts provide an arena for acknowledging what are sometimes isolating or tension-producing differences. For example, the artists in Teachers and Writers Collaborative in New York have pioneered dozens of ways of honoring the language skills of bi-lingual children. [16] Using these techniques, a poet asked bi-lingual children to talk about the words they loved best from Chinese, Spanish, and Hebrew. The words and phrases that came out of these talks were "given" to English-speaking children to write poems around. In this way, children who may have to struggle with the language of the classroom can shine.

Such turnabouts are in no way limited to the immediate members of a school community. In a Boston-area community, where there was an influx of Southeast Asian families, there began to develop considerable tension between Caucasian and Asian children. Teachers, who were quite concerned by the teasing and jeering, began teaching a unit on Asia, stressing the richness and diversity of Oriental culture. As one teacher recalls it, "The posters of palaces and sculptures were nice, they brightened up the room, but you could hardly say the kids made much sense of them. I think that the first break came when I was reading aloud some Vietnamese fairy tales. One of them was very much like Cinderella. A kid called out, "Hey, that's Cinderella, that's not from Vietnam, they borrowed it." When I suggested maybe it was the other way around, I think they were stunned. We talked about a lot of the things that came to Europe or America from the Orient. We also talked about the possibility that since people everywhere share a lot of the same hopes and fears, their stories might be very similar." [17]

The Philadelphia chapter of Young Audiences has found a way to cross the age barrier that usually separates the young and old in city neighborhoods. A series of their concerts brought together school children and elderly people from neighborhood daycare centers for senior citizens. Out of the original concerts a number of other contacts emerged. Young and old visit each other at lunch time, talk over the music they have heard, and the older people have begun to share their life histories.

Tired of "Sally, Dick, and Jane" and the Same Old Green Walls?

Many artist residencies culminate in a project or a performance that often leaves its stamp on the school. Some artists actively use the school setting as a part of their raw materials and work with students to redesign or add to it. For example, one architect spent time teaching children to think about their everyday surroundings and how they would change them if they could. Together, the architect and the kindergarten class took on the job of analyzing why the classroom seemed "dull and boring." After working on possible changes, the class decided to paint rainbow stripes around the blackboard and a portion of the walls. In a writing residency, third-graders worked on spicing up the early reading books provided for younger children. The zany "alphabeterrarium" on the facing page was the result.

Although exhibits and performances are shorter-lived than murals or permanent sculptures, they too can contribute to school life. Performances are often a source of tremendous pleasure and pride for students who take part in them, either as knowing members of the audience or as performers. These events provide ideal occasions for opening up the school to parents, other schools, and the larger community. In one school, a final dance performance was the occasion for inviting a nearby school for the deaf into

monstrous MURdring mushrooms
MARKeTing Marshmellows.

the public elementary school for the first time. So successful was the afternoon, that since then the two schools regularly exchange art exhibits and softball teams. Following the first residency in a rural school with no art program, a film-maker arranged a screening of his own and students' films. The afternoon before the showing, one of the teachers told the artist not to be upset if the show didn't draw much of a crowd. "Night-time events just aren't well attended." Chairs were set up for fifty. That evening an overflow crowd of 200 (from a total population of 1,100) filled the gym. The artist residencies in that community are now in their third year, sponsored by raffles, a local trust, and contributions from the school budget and state arts commission.

SUMMARY

You now have dozens of examples that illustrate what can happen if children are given a serious chance to participate in the arts. Behind all of these examples is a small, but powerful, set of reasons for providing children with arts experiences. Here are those reasons:

1. Art can "turn on" children to the pleasure and excitement of aesthetic experience, including:

—using their imaginations

—becoming wide awake to the world around them

—enjoying the originality, craft, and insight that is to be discovered in stories, paintings, dances, and films.

2. Art can underscore and enhance basic learning of all kinds. In learning to make and appreciate art, children can:

—learn fundamental symbol-using skills akin to those they depend on in reading, writing, and arithmetic

—have experience with the demanding processes of planning, drafting, editing, and polishing a work

—experiment with new ideas and concepts.

3. Art can build community spirit and cultural awareness. By watching or joining an arts project, children may:

—learn what it is to contribute to a community

—shake loose some of their stereotypic beliefs about other people: about students with different abilities, teachers, or children from different ethnic or cultural backgrounds

—realize the integrity of cultural traditions different from their own.

These points should give you a running start on answering the questions you want to examine. As an advocate for the arts in education, you may want to make different points with classroom teachers, parents, art specialists, or community business people who are thinking about making contributions. For some people, statements about the importance of aesthetic literacy carry a lot of weight. For others, discussions of imagination do not hold a candle to arguments about the role of the arts in bolstering basic education. Not only do you have to do some talking, you also have to listen and decide which examples and arguments will convince and which will annoy.

When you speak with people, concentrate on being direct, clear, and concrete. Talk with art and music teachers who have worked with children and the arts. They will be able to offer you samples of children's work or examples of the power and effectiveness of the arts in classroom settings. Arrange to interview a parent who is an artist. Ask him or her to describe several ways of learning or growing through the arts. Combine these classroom examples and adult quotes into a fact sheet, pamphlet, or display for the front hall of the school. In other words, now that you know what the arts are good for, go to it!

REFERENCES

While a list of arts-in-education publications is at the end of this book, the following list contains many specific references that relate to points made in the chapter. It is always helpful to have published material to back up your arguments about the importance of the arts in education, and this list contains some of the most important writing on the subject.

[1] For many examples of the flexibility and seriousness of artists' thought processes, see D. Perkins, *The Mind's Best Work* (Cambridge, Mass.: Harvard University Press, 1982); or M. Csikszentmihalyi and J.W. Getzels, "The Concern for Discovery: An Attitudinal Component of Creative Production," *Journal of Personality* 1970, *38 (1)*, pp. 90-105.

[2] A fine discussion of this kind of "thick" perception occurs in E. Winner, *Invented worlds: The psychology of the arts* (Cambridge, Mass.: Harvard University Press, 1982). Also see, M. Greene, "A Teacher Talks to Teachers: Perspectives on the Lincoln Center Institute" New York: Lincoln Center Institute Occasional Papers, No. 1, Fall, 1980.

[3] Basic information about the development of moral reasoning has often been collected by presenting individuals with imaginary situations and asking them to think through the issues from the perspective of one of the participants. See L. Kohlberg and C. Gilligan, "The Adolescent as a Philosopher: The Discovery of Self in a Post-Conventional World," *Daedalus* (Fall 1971): pp. 1051-1086.

Researchers and teachers are just beginning to examine the power of theatre to educate. The play by Carol Korty is a particularly powerful example of theatre specifically designed to encourage children to think about social and personal issues. Together, Korty and Young Audiences of Massachusetts developed a set of educational experiences tied to the production of the play, which ranged from history classes to discussions of parallel issues in the actors' own lives.

[4] In his article, "Why Metaphors Are Necessary And Not Just Nice," *Educational Theory* 25, pp. 45-53), Andrew Ortony discusses how frequent and important figurative language is to thinking and communication, even outside the context of poetry.

[5] See H. Gardner; E. Winner & M. Kircher's article, "Children's Conceptions of the Arts," *Journal of Aesthetic Education* 9, (3), pp. 60-77.

[6] Artists' autobiographies provide us with clear evidence about the early and lasting effects of growing up in settings where art is thought of as important rather than "just nice." See B. Goldovsky, *My Road to Opera* (Boston: Houghton-Mifflin, 1979). Laura Chapman's book, *Instant Art, Instant Culture* (New York: Teachers College Press, 1982) discusses the reluctance on the part of American educators to provide early, continuous, serious art instruction in the schools.

[7] There is a strong analogy between artistic literacy and computer literacy. Increasingly, middle-class children learn about keyboards, commands, and information by playing games and experimenting on family calculators and computers. Children without those advantages will be "left out," through no fault of their own, if schools do not elect to make computer literacy available to all

students. Similarly, when schools do not elect to make aesthetic literacy widely available, only those children who are provided with piano lessons, trips to museums, and tickets to performances will have the advantage of growing up aesthetically aware.

[8] An example of this kind of training is discussed in J. Silverman, E. Winner, A. Rosenstiel, and H. Gardner, "On Training Sensitivity to Painting Styles." *Perception* 4, pp. 373-384.

[9] An overview of the contribution of artistic activity to early symbolic development can be found in D. Wolf and H. Gardner, *Early Symbolization, New Directions for Child Development* (San Francisco: Jossey-Bass, 1979).

[10] The number of studies that indicate the contributions of specific artistic skills to particular basic skills are mounting. For example, researchers now understand the contribution of drawing skills to early writing. Two of the best studies in this area are: M. Clay, *What Did I Write?* (Auckland, New Zealand: Heinemann, 1975); and D. Graves, *Balance the Basics: Let Them Write* (New York: Ford Foundation, 1978). The influence of early exposure to books and reading on language learning is reported in C. Chomsky, *The Acquisition of Syntax in Children 5 to 10* (Cambridge, Mass: MIT Press, 1969).

[11] See R. Arnheim, *The Genesis of a Painting: Piccasso's Guernica* (Berkeley: University of California Press, 1962). The poet Randall Jarrell describes the slow and careful processes involved in writing poetry in his book, *Jerome: The Biography of a Poem* (New York: Grossman, 1971).

[12] See E. Richardson, *In the Early World* (New York: Pantheon Books, 1964).

[13] The film, "Statues hardly ever smile" emerged from this project. It was the collaborative effort of Brooklyn School District 17, the Brooklyn Arts and Cultural Association, and the Brooklyn Museum. A similar collaboration between schools and museums is the ongoing "Learning to Read through the Arts Programs, Inc.," that operates under the auspices of the Solomon R. Guggenheim Museum (4 E. 70th Street, New York, New York 10021).

[14] See J. Eddy, "The Case for the Arts in Schools", Report No. 7 from The Arts, Education, and Americans, Inc., New York, New York.

[15] See J. Remer, *Changing Schools through the Arts: The Power of an Idea* (New York: McGraw-Hill Book Co., 1982).

[16] See B. Zavatsky and R. Padgett, *The Whole Word Catalogue 2* (New York: Teachers and Writers, Inc., 1977).

[17] Richard Lewis, working at the Touchstone Center in New York, has produced a number of books and materials that illustrate the integrity of other cultures and the themes that bind people of all cultures together. Particularly powerful is his collection of children's writings from around the world, *Miracles* (New York: Simon and Schuster, 1966).

Chapter 2
Meeting the Players – The Who of Arts in Education

by Thomas Wolf and Polly Price

"If we can only find a really good performing group, a talented visual artist, and a poet for our arts-in-education program, we will be off and running." This statement may be true, at least as far as it goes. But the poet, the visual artist, and the performing group by themselves will not be able to guarantee success; nor will they be able to make sure that arts-in-education activities continue at the school. These outside artistic professionals are only one part of a team that involves teachers, school administrators, students, parents, and others. Each group has a hand in determining just how successful the program will be.

This chapter introduces the people who are involved in arts-in-education activities. Some of the people play a major role — like the school superintendent who recommends the expenditure of funds or the dancer who plans and carries out the program; others play only a peripheral role — like the school secretary who types the press releases or the parent who attends the final performance. But it is essential to know who the various players are, what they do, and what can be expected of them. It is also necessary to learn how to develop their cooperation and support so that this year's program will go smoothly and will be continued and expanded next year.

Who Are the School Players?

Schools consist of eight distinct groups of people who contribute to the success or failure of an arts-in-education program. They are:

—school board members
—superintendents
—principals
—classroom teachers
—arts specialists
—other school staff
—students
—parents

While certain schools will not have representatives from every group (private schools will not have school board members and superintendents; some small public schools will not have arts specialists), most will be found in the great majority of schools. What do these people do? And what steps should be taken to encourage their interest and support?

The School Board or School Committee

This is the group of locally elected officials that determines the overall policies and budgets of the school system in accordance with state and federal laws. Accountable to parents and other voters in the community, school board members have to be sensitive to public opinion. The business of the school board member includes responding to concerns about the lack of discipline, the need to prepare youngsters for the working world, or declining College Board scores. While many school board members acknowledge the importance of the arts, they must place the arts in the context of other competing priorities.

Since the school board has the power of the purse, it is important to see that board members give more than lip-service support to arts programs. There are several strategies in developing this support for the arts:

—First, find out if some school board members are affiliated with arts organizations. Does a member serve as a trustee of the museum or symphony for example? This is a tip-off that he or she may be sympathetic.

—Second, determine whether there are any state or federal laws or guidelines that suggest that the arts should play a basic role in education. For example, some state boards of education have a stated policy on arts education requiring schools to teach art or music. In a specific case, a federal judge in Boston in 1975 wrote into a desegregation order that schools should use the resources of the city's museums and performing arts organizations in the ongoing curriculum.

The Superintendent

This man or woman is the top administrator of the school system and the head of the professional staff. The superintendent is responsible for recommending policy and budget to the school board and for seeing that the board's decisions are implemented. Because the superintendent often carries much influence with the school board and supervises the carrying out of curriculum in individual schools, his or her personal interest in the arts can be very important to the success and even the existence of artist residencies and performances. A good word from the superintendent can result in an allotment for arts-in-education in the school system's budget. The superintendent can also help along an already scheduled residency. In a city in New Hampshire, for example, a dance troupe was having difficulty scheduling residence activities. Performances lasted longer than the normal class periods and dancers also wanted uninterrupted blocks of time to do intensive dance training. Fortunately, the superintendent was a dance enthusiast and understood the rare opportunity the residency offered for "a different kind of learning." He issued a mandate that "when the dancers are here, we go on dance time" and schedules were adjusted accordingly.

A superintendent is usually interested in programs that have been successful in other school systems, particularly if they appear to have some potential for replication. Therefore, one way to approach a superintendent is with documentation of arts-in-education programs that have been successful elsewhere. There are many aspects of the program that will be of interest to the superintendent — program quality, funding, involvement of principals and teachers, parental and community support. Documentation of other programs should include information on all of these aspects. The superintendent has a large constituency to please and any approach will be more successful if it has the support of a broad spectrum of the community both within and outside the school.

The Principal

For an arts program in a particular school, the principal is often *the* key to success. If the principal thinks the program is a frill or, worse, a big headache, it can falter or fail. In one New England elementary school, students were energetically working on a ceramic mural, which required that they carry buckets of water from their classrooms past the principal's office to the mural site. As one of the students was walking past the principal's office, the principal happened to be meeting with a community businessman who had come to complain about student vandalism and a general lack of discipline. When the businessman saw the student running through the halls with a bucket of water and going outside during class hours, the principal became extremely angry and told the supervising teacher that the activity would have to stop immediately.

On the other hand, a principal's interest in arts-in-education can be a special blessing. It is often the principal who controls schedules and resources and it is he or she who can "make exceptions" to certain rules. In one case, an elementary school principal joined a team of teachers from his school on a museum visit in order to plan an integrated social studies curriculum. When the group arrived, the museum director asked the principal whether he might enjoy a special guided tour of the collection including a behind-the-scenes look at how exhibits were prepared. After an hour of conversation, the two men found they had much in common: each was responsible for maintaining a staff, each faced budget cuts, each felt pressure from above to be a better manager. With growing respect for the museum director, the principal also found his interest in collaboration growing. When the teachers presented their curriculum plan to the principal, they had his support.

Winning over a principal to arts-in-education programs may be as easy as convincing him or her that such programs will make the school a "special place." Not only can the arts enliven the school program and brighten up the physical environment, but they may be one tool for tackling some particular priority within the school. As we noted in Chapter 1, the arts may contribute to students' sensitivity toward cultural and racial diversity or they may bolster basic education. It is important to find out areas of particular priority to the school principal and to focus some of the arguments for arts-in-education programs within that context.

Classroom Teachers

While it may be the superintendent or principal who determines whether an arts-in-education program comes into a school, it is more often the classroom teacher who can determine its success with the students. Classroom teachers can be enthusiastic and supportive; they can work to develop activities that immediately precede or follow up a performance or residency. But the pressures on them to carry out their own teaching activities may make them less than enthusiastic about yet another activity that competes for teaching time. A sixth-grade teacher expressed it this way: "With the hundreds of other pressures on us, we are expected to instill everything from good manners to good grammar. There isn't one of us who doesn't enjoy the luxury of 'extras' like arts and artists in the classroom, but many of us feel we simply cannot spare the time. The solution is for artists and teachers to work on residencies and other activities together. That way it is clear that we have many of the same goals."

Before a performance or residency begins, classroom teachers can generate readiness and enthusiasm with books, discussions, or films. After the artist leaves, the lasting effects of arts exposure are also determined by

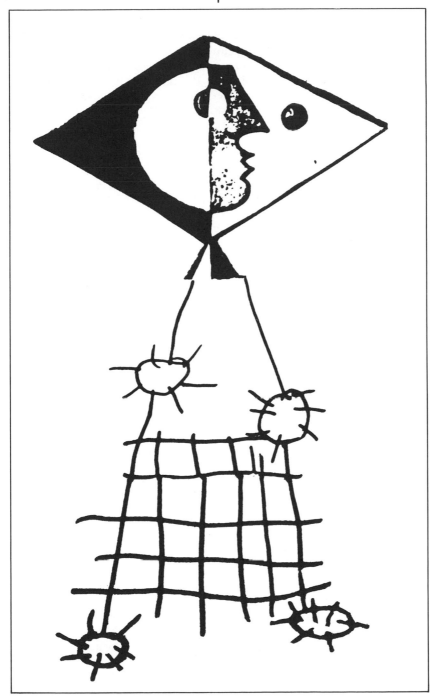

classroom teachers. Students can be told they must "get right back to work" or they can be encouraged to assimilate the arts experience into their thoughts and their activities. Because of this crucial role, it is essential that classroom teachers are involved in the planning of arts-in-education activities. Their educational goals should be respected and activities should be designed that feed into teachers' teaching agendas.

Arts Specialists

In addition to classroom teachers, many schools have arts specialists who teach music, visual arts, dance, or theatre. The relationship between these teachers and the incoming arts professionals is particularly sensitive. The opportunity for competition is obvious. If an art teacher is dealing with painting on an ongoing basis and a painter comes in to do a painting residency, it may be unclear to students and to others in the school community what is really going on. Is there something wrong with the art teacher? Does he or she lack adequate skill to deal with the activity?

Arts specialists also may have another worry on their minds. School systems may try to get around the expense of an ongoing art or music program by bringing in outside artistic professionals. The logic appears to be that the school can save money by having artists in residence instead of having art teachers and can achieve arts exposure without carrying full salaries plus benefits. But as most teachers know, the art or music teacher and the incoming artist or performer serve very different functions that complement one another. Art teachers provide *ongoing* training to students; artists show students how professional artists think and work.

Arts specialists should be consulted rather than bypassed in the planning of arts-in-education programs. They know what the students have been exposed to, what activities they have tackled and which have worked, and what has interested students. All of this is crucial information for artists and performers if their programs are going to link into the experience of the students.

Other School Staff

Schools have secretaries, custodians, nurses, and cooks, all of whom can help make an arts-in-education program successful. The following story illustrates some payoffs to good relationships with the entire school staff:

> Early in her residency an artist established a strong rapport with the school custodian who had initially been concerned about the children "making messes." Artist and custodian became the best of friends. Some months into the residency, the artist planned a

special ceremony at which a children's mural would be unveiled for the community. As part of the fund-raising event, the artist agreed to hang some of her work in the school lobby. As she began installing her abstract, cubist impressions of prone nude figures, a school board member who was walking by suggested that the art be removed before it could be observed by the children. The custodian was quite upset and rose to the defense of the artist: "This woman is an artist and that is a piece of art. They have as much place in this school as I do. So, if the art goes, I have to go too." The school board member was surprised and impressed and the art work stayed on the wall.

School staff members can be important to an arts-in-education activity, but it is impossible to involve them in all the details of the planning process. Nevertheless, there are simple forms of courtesy that should be followed. All school staff should receive basic information about the upcoming activities through a simple memo that outlines schedules, equipment and space requirements, and proposed activities. In addition, any member of the school staff who will be expected to carry out some task related to the project (from unlocking doors to typing press releases) should be spoken to well in advance by a person in charge. After the person performs the task, he or she should be thanked. In particular, staff members will appreciate a word of thanks from artists and performers who are, after all, the "stars of the show."

Students

Making generalizations about students is difficult. They come in all sizes and shapes, from different social, ethnic, and racial backgrounds, with different sets of talents and skills. Some have physical or intellectual disabilities; others have emotional difficulties; some are excited by the school program, others are bored. One child may be the daughter of a cellist; the girl beside her may never have been exposed to live music of any kind.

When planning arts-in-education programs, it is vital to remember three things that all students share. First, up until late high school age, students do not have a choice about attending school. In that sense, they are a captive audience. This is an important consideration for artists and performers who work in schools. One of their tasks is to overcome an attitude among some students that since school attendance is required, not chosen, then anything that happens in school is an obligation not an opportunity. Second, many students expect that much of what happens during an artist's residency will be like a geography or science class — questions and answers, quizzes, worksheets, and grades. Third, because they are young, students' minds, like their bodies, are growing at a rapid rate. Underneath the boredom and reserve, there is much to work with.

These three facts lead to three important considerations in planning:

—Is the arts activity going to be required of students or chosen by them? There are arguments pro and con on this subject. Some people feel that students need to be exposed to something in order to know enough to make an informed choice about whether they want to participate. Others feel that arts activities are more fruitful when they are offered to students who really care about them. There is no right answer, but it is important to design the program with a sensitivity toward whether the audience is "captive" or "free."

—Is the arts activity going to be highly structured or more free-form? Artists tend to like the latter, but they should be realistic about the fact that students are probably used to structured activities and may need direction and supervision in adjusting to less structured situations that stress invention rather than information.

—Is the program or performance going to be the same one that played before the Rotary and senior citizens or is it specially tuned to capitalize on younger people's attention spans, basic curiosities, and interests? (Chapter 4 discusses how this "tuning" can occur.)

Parents

Parents are often the unsung heroes and heroines of arts-in-education programs. Frequently it is parental pressure (and sometimes even money) that makes these programs possible. Whether or not parents are involved in the day-to-day operation of the school (and this will vary from school to school), they can form a very strong lobby in support of the arts. It is essential to inform and involve parents in the planning and implementation of arts programs. If there is an active parents' organization, its members can help the school community raise funds, find supplies, host exhibit openings, or make presentations to the school board and other organizations.

There are many steps that can be taken to assure broad parental involvement in arts-in-education activities. Meetings about such activities should be held on a regular basis, parents should be notified well ahead of time, and a group of parents should do telephone follow-up to encourage attendance. In addition, there should be some component of every arts-in-education program to which parents can come such as a performance or an exhibition. The timing of this event should be carefully scheduled to encourage good attendance. Parents can also be encouraged to be a part of the activities. They can help make costumes for a theatrical performance or they can hang paintings for an exhibition. Finally, parents can become involved in follow-up activities with their own children, particularly if artists and teachers prepare some material suggesting things that they can do. These might include trips to a museum, attendance at concerts, or specific activities that can be done at home.

What Do School People Want?

An arts-in-education program can be a great asset to a school. But it also places great burdens on everyone involved. Schedules must be adjusted, space must be found, resources (both financial and human) must be secured, and, in some cases, reluctant people must be convinced of the program's ultimate value. This being the case, it is essential that certain steps be followed to gain the cooperation of school personnel:

1. School personnel should be treated as professionals who have good ideas and insights to contribute to arts-in-education program planning. Many have an interest in and knowledge about the arts that should not be ignored. Most know a great deal about planning activities for children.

2. If school personnel are expected to spend extra time in arts-in-education planning, they should either be given release time to do so or should receive extra compensation. Most of them are already overworked and it is unreasonable to expect them to welcome yet another responsibility without adjustments in their schedules or pay.

3. Every attempt should be made to connect the arts-in-education program to the ongoing curriculum. In this way, the program can assist and supplement rather than compete with regular in-school activities.

4. Every member of the school staff should be informed in writing well in advance about the mechanics of the arts-in-education program: date(s), time(s), students involved, space to be used, activities planned. Nothing should come as a surprise.

5. Everyone who is to be involved in the arts program should be told very specifically what is expected of them. School personnel plan their schedules well in advance and do not welcome spur-of-the-moment arrangements that require last-minute adjustments in their plans.

Sensitivity to the needs of school personnel will inevitably reap great rewards when an arts-in-education program is presented at the school. Artists and performers should be fully briefed on their role in making sure the collaboration goes smoothly. They must be told that a good performance or a successful residency activity is only a part of their task. Another part involves diplomacy and sensitivity in working with the school community.

Who Are the Arts People?

Artists have been trained to dance, act, paint or play music very well. They take this activity seriously, so seriously in some cases that they have made tremendous personal sacrifices to be artists. *The most important overall*

need of an artist working in a school is to have his or her skills and needs taken seriously. This is not always easy. A school needs to teach many skills in addition to artistic ones. School personnel have to juggle the needs of classroom teachers, specialists, the athletic department — as well as artists. It is sometimes difficult to satisfy an artist who seems to be saying, "What I do is the *only* thing that is really important."

Since most artists and performers have been out of school for a long time, they simply do not know the routines, the layout, or the rules. Many artists can tell you an unhappy "first-day-on-the-job" story. Performers maintain that it is not unusual to arrive at a school and find that no one seems to know why they are there. Almost always there is a simple explanation for the misunderstanding — the front desk had not been informed, or the event represents a last-minute change in the schedule. But to artists unfamiliar with schools, it is very disorienting.

On the other hand, artists can seem too demanding. "The performers waited for absolute silence before they would play a note," said one teacher, describing a string quartet performance for a junior high school. "Sure it is important to be quiet in order to listen to music, but the musicians seemed to have no sense for just how quiet the kids were, given their usual level of activity." "You might think that sculptor's tools were made of gold the way he screamed at me when I picked one up to look at it," one student related. But these demands and quirks of temperament usually stem from a very simple need: artists and performers, like the rest of us, want to be admired and taken seriously.

What Else Do Artists and Performers Need?

Beyond being taken seriously, the other needs of artists and performers center around the following things:

- facilities
- supplies and equipment
- reasonable student group size
- teacher and / or parent assistance
- planning time
- preparation of school community
- "sanity" time

— Facilities

Every artist and performer has space requirements that should be carefully checked. Some performing troupes will perform almost anywhere, others, such as dancers, may require that a performing space be clear of all obstructions, have a wood floor, and be heated to at least 65 degrees. If a school cannot provide such a space, it should not hire a group that requires it. A visual artist, particularly one who will be working in the school for several weeks, may require a lockable studio space with adequate ventilation and some natural light. If the only thing available is a broom closet, plans should not proceed until an attempt has been made to negotiate with the artist. Sometimes an artist can be very accommodating if he or she knows the situation in advance. If the artist cannot adjust to the available space and if no other space can be found, then another activity or another artist should be chosen.

—Supplies and Equipment

Artists and performers may also require certain supplies and equipment that should be specified in writing before any kind of agreement is signed. Musicians may require a tuned piano or music stands; artists may require paint, paper, clay, a kiln, or video equipment. Sometimes school administrators or parent-planners agree to provide these things before they really know where they will find them or how they will pay for them. This can lead to trouble. When the artist or performer arrives, he or she is put in the awkward situation of making a scene or making do with inadequate materials. "It is a no-win situation," says one artist. "How can you scream and yell on the first day of the residency and permanently sour your relationships with teachers and students? Yet you know perfectly well that things are not going to go well if you do not have the things you were promised."

—Student Group Size

"Participatory drama for groups of 200 kids or less per show" — so reads the first line of a theatre group's brochure. The group's show has been carefully designed so that it "works" for up to 200 students. Yet in almost a third of the schools in which this troupe has performed, group size has been a problem. "I understand the schools' dilemma," says one of the actors. "They have a limited budget and they want to squeeze as many kids into the performances as they can. But our show is not like a baseball game. We cannot simply jam in more people and give the same quality spectacle, particularly since student participation is what we are about. It is more like sitting down to a meal. The more people that sit down to a single dish of ice cream, the less each person will get."

In the case of performances, the number of students that can effectively participate depends on many factors. Small puppets are most effective in an intimate setting; some choral and theatrical groups work best in a larger environment. The artist or performer is the professional who knows the optimum situation and should communicate with the school about the best way to achieve it. Sometimes the honest desire to have all students benefit from the performance can be achieved in other ways. Multiple performances, performances in alternative spaces, or video and / or sound recordings are some ways to build flexibility into performance formats.

—Teacher and Parent Assistance

The best kinds of arts-in-education experiences are those in which an incoming artist has the benefit of working together with one or more teachers. This often happens when teachers have participated in the decision to bring a particular artist or performer into the school. Yet there may be times when teachers cannot or do not wish to be involved. In such cases, parent volunteers can join in. They can transport equipment, supplies, even kids; they can also take on the role of teaching assistant; or they can even make an enthusiastic audience. In some cases, participating teachers may want parents to join in and assist with the residency activities, and this should certainly be encouraged.

—Preparation of School Community

It is wonderful to know that everyone in the school — students, teachers, administrators, janitorial staff, parents — has been told "the artists are coming." It is even better when the entire school community has been told why they are coming and what they will be doing. Everyone should be briefed on the artists and the upcoming activities *and* informed of any special needs of the guests. The percussion player may need some help getting his tympani to the gymnasium. The painter will need the time from 2 to 4 in the afternoon as his own personal studio work time. Anyone who can bring egg and milk cartons in for the sculpture residency will be helping out. Artists and performers want to feel a part of a community that appreciates them and is willing to help out. The reward for informing people — whether through the school newspaper, notes to parents, or word of mouth — is more successful events and more contented artists, teachers, students, and parents.

—"Sanity" Time

Perhaps the greatest tension that can arise in connection with artists' visits revolves around conflicting attitudes toward work and pay. If teachers can teach from 8:10 a.m. to 3:20 p.m., why should a poet be paid $150 for a "work day" that involves four 45-minute classes? Pressure is often put on artists and performers to "do a full day's work for a full day's pay." Nothing could be more detrimental to an effective residency than putting artists and performers in this situation. They need creative time to think, to practice, to plan. The nature of their work is often intense and exhausting. They need their "sanity" time, but a coffee break may not be adequate. Squeezing a little more work out of an artist may lead to getting a lot less quality out of the program.

WHO SHOULD BE HIRED?

Selecting an individual artist or a group of artists is a difficult process that should proceed on two fronts at once. Everyone interested in the arts-in-education program should as a matter of course collect information on artists and performers who might provide outstanding activities for young people. But at the same time the search must be informed by a consideration of those design options that will give the school the best program for the available budget.

What are some of these program options? While more will be said on this topic in Chapter 4, some specific considerations that are relevant in artist and performer selection are listed below:

— Is the school looking for short- or long-term programs? Would it be more valuable to bring a single artist in for an extended period or use the same financial resources to have several short-term contacts with a variety of outside artists?

— What art forms should be represented? Do teachers want a poet, a composer, an instrumentalist, a dancer, an actor, a painter, a sculptor, a craftsperson, a media artist? The answer to this question will depend on budget constraints, teacher interest, curriculum questions, facilities, and the school's past history with particular art forms.

— Which additional educational elements would be desirable as a part of the program: teacher workshops, community workshops, field trips, or weekend activities for students and parents? Artists vary in their interest and ability to direct or become involved in these activities.

— What are other schools in the area considering and is there a possibility of getting a reduced "block-booking" or "extended residency" fee from an artist or performer if various schools work together? Keep in mind that when artists have to travel a long distance for relatively short-term work, it is often desirable for them to offer a special reduced fee for a longer period of employment. Joint planning of this kind in the New England region has saved tens of thousands of dollars over the past five years.

—What limitations or opportunities are posed by funding realities? Is it possible to secure more money for certain types of activities than for others? While activities should not be planned solely around financial resources, sometimes an element can be designed into a program that will lead to additional income. For example, one school system built a "senior citizen" component into an artist residency and secured a large amount of funding that helped pay for other aspects of the program.

—What is the temperament and character of the school? What kind of performance or residency will work best given the background and interests of the school community? For example, if there is an active band program, workshops by a brass group would be effective. If the school has a strong program in math and computer science, perhaps a composer utilizing a computer / synthesizer or a media artist utilizing sophisticated technology might fit in well.

Artist Selection Criteria

The actual selection of the artist or performer involves careful scrutiny of many things:

—*the quality of his or her work* (Is this someone who has clearly shown great skill at the chosen artistic occupation?)

—*communication skills* (How well does the artist communicate ideas and concepts about the art form?)

—*personality* (Is this someone who will get on well with the students, teachers, and others in the school community?)

—*working style* (The environment of the school can be a demanding place to work. Does the artist's working style show a flexibility to accommodate these difficulties?)

—*motivation for working in schools* (Is the artist or performer really interested in working in schools or does he or she view the invitation simply as an opportunity to earn some money?)

—*goals for the arts program* (Teachers and administrators designing the total curriculum for the school have hopes and ideas about what a residency, performance, or series of workshops can accomplish. Does the artist or performer under consideration offer activities and experiences that will support and enhance these educational objectives?)

—*experience in working with students* (Great artists and performers can be frightened or bored by young people for whom the arts are not the "be all and end all." Check carefully to make sure the ones being considered have had some prior positive experience working with the same age group that they propose to work with in the school.)

WHERE DO YOU FIND OUT ABOUT ARTISTS AND PERFORMERS?

Many people hire artists and performers by looking through flyers and brochures sent to them in the mail. These same people would never think of buying a new appliance for their homes without checking out several models and several stores. They have learned that all advertising must be taken with a grain of salt.

Some years ago, the chairperson of a school's Parent Arts Committee showed the publicity brochure of a performing group to her mother, who had served on the same committee years before. "Fascinating," said her mother, "I think I have an old brochure from the same company from fifteen years ago." Indeed she did. The brochure had not changed a bit. There were the same impressive reviews, the same descriptive paragraph announcing "an exciting new program for schools."

This shows how important it is to go beyond publicity in gaining information about artists and performers. There are four additional ways that schools can find out about them:

1. School representatives can view artists in action.
2. They can talk to others who have engaged artists in the past.
3. They can ask artists for additional information such as letters of reference, a resume, press clippings, or a portfolio.
4. They can interview artists.

The most reliable way to form a judgment is to see an artist in a situation as much like the one being contemplated as possible. Seeing painters at work in their studios, for example, is not the same as seeing them in a school situation. An actress in an exciting one-woman show at a downtown theatre will not necessarily do a terrific job in a performance for junior high schoolers. By the same token, just because someone on the Arts Committee was excited by the courses offered by a recognized sculptor at a professional arts school, does not mean that this same sculptor will provide a meaningful and exciting residency for elementary school children. If people are going to make the effort to go out and see artists and performers in action, they should take a little bit more time to look for the performance or residency situation that will tell the most about how the artist will do in the proposed residency setting.

Since no one person can ever review all the artists and performers that are available, many schools and parent-teacher organizations have organized themselves into consortia that enable many individuals to share the work of evaluating artists. In one such consortium in New England, representatives from twenty-six separate schools each take responsibility for reviewing the work of two or three artists. Added to these evaluations are their observations of artists and performers working in their respective schools during the current year. Sharing this material allows any one school to have a rich library of detailed information on the work of artists and performers. (More will be said about such word-of-mouth networking in Chapter 3.)

Interviewing an artist often gives a good sense of how experienced, flexible, personable, and effective he or she will be in a school situation. It is usually unfair to demand an interview with someone who will only be coming into the school for a single workshop or performance. However, if a more extended residency is planned, an interview is essential. A few tips may be useful:

—The teacher(s) who will be most involved with the artist or performer should conduct the interview or be involved in it. The dynamic between artists and teachers is crucial.

—Someone who is experienced in interviewing should conduct the interview or be present to make sure it goes smoothly. Remember, the artist or performer is also forming an impression of the school community.

—Do not be confrontational; it proves nothing. You can get the same information by judging the artist's responses to probing yet friendly questions.

—Make a list of the questions you feel should be covered before the interview begins.

—Do not waste the time of artists or performers whom you know you will not hire.

(Once again, more information on this phase of the process is covered in Chapter 3.)

HOW CAN TEACHERS AND ARTISTS DEVELOP A GOOD WORKING RELATIONSHIP?

"I knew things were getting bad when the teacher at the school where I was doing my residency asked me to grade some essays that her students had written about art." (An artist)

"It made me angry when the artist we had brought in to do a residency program came into my science class and started telling kids what was wrong with their drawings of bean seedlings." (A teacher)

These two comments reveal one of the most difficult problems in implementing a successful school arts program: forging a good working relationship between artists and teachers. Unfortunately, there is ample opportunity for misunderstandings, hostility, and distrust between regular teaching staff in a school and artists who are "outsiders." It is, first and foremost, crucial to make sure that everyone knows that the incoming professionals are there to *supplement*, not replace, the regular school program and personnel.

It is equally important to clarify precisely what it is fair to expect from both sides and to set limits on what each can ask of the other. Artists are not members of the regular teaching staff and should not be expected to cover study halls. Teachers are not stage managers or janitors and they should not be expected to move stage sets or clean up the art room after a painting session. One artist remembers the first discussion she had with a principal at the beginning of a six-week residency. "Oh, and by the way," he said as they were finishing the discussion, "faculty meetings are from 3 to 5 on Wednesdays. See you there. I want you to let our teachers know just when and how you can help out if things get tight around here." A performer recalls the times he had to perform for large groups of children while their teachers were absent, taking a coffee or a smoke break. "You become a policeman, not a performer. And because the teachers aren't there to see and hear what we are doing, there is no follow-up in the classroom."

Similarly, a teacher found herself in the awkward situation of having to develop residency-related teaching materials on very short notice: "It is not that I did not fully support the program; but I simply did not have adequate preparation time for the task and I resented the attitude that I was insensitive and unsupportive when I questioned whether the request was appropriate." To facilitate mutual understanding, teachers and artists need adequate opportunity for informal discussion. If face-to-face meetings cannot be arranged, a phone call or two should be an absolute requirement. If either side detects a problem in advance, it can be attended to and solved before the pressure of the actual school activities shorten people's tempers and patience.

The longer the period in which an artist or performer is going to work in the school, the more he or she should be expected to find out about and support the work of the teachers in the school. Art and music teachers can often capitalize on the ideas of an outside professional to reinforce something that they have been working on with students. An interesting example of this occurred a number of years ago when a Boston-based woodwind quintet was hired to undertake a series of band workshops in Maine high schools:

> In one of the schools, the band teacher met and talked with the performers in advance and told them how much difficulty he was having getting the students to breathe properly. "They simply do not concentrate on their breathing and so we lose sound at the end of phrases and everything goes flat. Anything you can do would be a help." When the residency began, the flutist asked several students to come forward and demonstrate how they would pitch a baseball. When the first student began his wind-up, complete with arm and

leg motion, the flutist shouted, "Stop! You pitch with your arm don't you? Why are you throwing with your leg?" The student explained that he was going through a wind-up. "What's winding up?" the flutist asked. The student explained that he had to prepare his body so that he could get his full weight behind the pitch. "Do you wind-up when you play your instrument?" the flutist asked. The student appeared puzzled, so the flutist demonstrated the correct way to breathe, likening it to the pitcher's wind-up. "I call it a 'breathe-up,'" he said. "You know, we wind players have to prepare our bodies too before we play or we won't make it to the end of the musical line." For the next half hour, all the wind players in the band worked on breathing excercises. "It was amazing," the band teacher said a year later. "That demonstration did great things for the band. Everyone told me afterwards that the band was sounding so good and it was because those musicians reinforced for the kids how important it was to breathe correctly."

When artists or performers come into a school situation, they carry the mantle of "experts." It takes a teacher with a lot of self-confidence to use this situation to advantage and not to feel threatened by it. For artists and performers who have been classroom teachers and have worked both sides of a residency program, there is usually great sensitivity to the problem. Said one art teacher: "You better believe I resented being treated like I was 'just a teacher' and it was the artist who really knew what she was talking about. Damn it, I had done residencies too. But somehow in the school where I was an art *teacher*, this didn't count." Clearly, teachers are experts too. They know the school, the kids, their curriculum, and what kinds of activities will work best in a given situation. Artists from the outside should do all they can to support them.

HOW CAN THE ARTIST BE MADE A PART OF THE COMMUNITY?

There once was an artist (named Bill) who was an amateur ice hockey player. He was also an avid ice hockey fan who had season tickets to his home-town professional hockey team games. Bill was hired to do a residency program in a community several miles from his home. Since he was in the school three consecutive days each week, he accepted an invitation from a family to make their house his home during his residency days. In that family was a fourteen-year-old athlete, John, who thought the arts were "stupid." During their times together, Bill and John would talk hockey. After several weeks, Bill asked John and his family whether they would have any interest in going to a hockey game with him. They jumped at the chance. That weekend, they took a bus to the town where Bill lived, visited Bill at his studio, and went to the hockey game with him. But while they were at Bill's studio, a strange thing happened. John watched Bill stretch canvases, set up a still life, and mix paints. He watched Bill paint and was impressed with the intensity with which he worked. Some weeks later the family returned to visit Bill. This time they went to a museum. A year later, John organized a most unusual senior trip with Bill's help. The seniors came to the city where Bill lived for a weekend; on Saturday night they went to a hockey game, on Sunday they went to a museum.

Perhaps the most important aspect of this story is not that an arts program made new converts for the arts but the way in which the conversion took place. Had the artist simply put in time at the school, chances are that he and John would never have met and certainly not have had the opportunity to talk about ice hockey. However, because the artist became a part of the community, lived and ate with a family, and met people in an informal way, it was possible to achieve several objectives of the school arts program outside of school.

How can this kind of experience be fostered? One way is to organize some residencies and workshops with artists and performers who will live in the community. While it may be difficult to organize housing situations in which bed *and* board are provided, local restaurants may contribute meal coupons. (With performers who have eating schedules that differ from the norm, this may be advantageous anyway.) As a general rule of thumb, an artist or performer should be housed in a place where privacy can be assured — a quiet room is a necessity and a private bath is desirable. There are some organizations that feel so strongly about the importance of artists and performers living with community families, that they only hire those who are willing to do so.

Using community locations can also serve to integrate the artist into the community. A senior citizen center, a community settlement house, even a bank lobby, may be appropriate for certain kinds of activities. This not only allows more people to enjoy the program, but it also lays the groundwork for fund-raising efforts. In addition, the very fact that artists and performers are out in the community will cause more people to hear about the program and be willing to support it.

Artists and performers may also be willing to promote the arts-in-education program by speaking on the radio, television, before civic clubs, and other gatherings. However, be sure to check out just how effective the artists or performers are as public speakers. Do not put them in a situation that you and they will regret. (Chapter 5 gives some examples of how performers have been used in public-speaking situations to drum up support for arts programs.)

Be sure to get clearance from the artists and performers before any final arrangements are made. If an extensive community residency is planned, this should be discussed in full and outlined in any contractual agreement. If a community person decides to set up some activities after the contract with the artists or performers has been signed, the proposed activities will have to be discussed and approved by them before plans are completed. They will have to be satisfied that the facilities are adequate and that the proposed activities will not be excessively difficult. Finally, if community-based events are planned, someone besides the artists or performers must agree to be on-site at the time of the event to assist in set-up, communication with the various people involved in the event, and other matters. It is unfair to ask artists to attend to small details of administration when so many other things must be looked after.

Collaborations between schools and artists are as tricky as they are important and rewarding. Their success depends largely on the ability of diverse people to work together. Many artists do not feel entirely comfortable in schools; and the school community does not always know exactly what to do with artists and performers who in many repsects are outsiders.

For this reason, it is often advisable to have someone who is sensitive both to the needs of schools and artists to make sure the arrangements for the proposed in-school activities go smoothly. Many programs, such as the Artists-in-Education program of the National Endowment for the Arts, have coordinators that provide this important liaison work. Even so, misunderstandings and difficult situations can arise. Says one experienced arts programmer: "I have a love / hate relationship with artists and performers. Sometimes they make my life so miserable that I vow never to work with them again. Then the next day they cause something so extraordinary to happen to my kids that I am in heaven. It never seems to be halfway and I am sure if it was, the program wouldn't be nearly as good."

Chapter 3
Building the Arts Program from A to Z

by Polly Price and Thomas Wolf

Cellist Natalie Bergman and painter Sylvan Smith agree that doing an arts program at the Bennett Elementary School is one of the great pleasures of their professional lives. "It's a breeze," says Sylvan. "People really have their act together," is Natalie's observation. Both agree that if working in the schools was *always* so satisfying, they would spend more of their time doing it. "But then there are some other schools that are very different. They are examples of the rule that if anything *can* go wrong, it *will* go wrong. But Bennett seems to know the secret of planning the residency from A to Z. Other schools should learn from them."

This chapter reveals the secrets of success at the Bennett School. The main reason that their arts programs always go well is that the teachers, administrators, parents, and students are all willing to work hard, attend to every detail, and make sure that nothing is left to chance. This chapter tells what they do and how they do it. It is written for anyone interested in the mechanics of building an arts-in-education program and getting it permanently established in a school.

FINDING ARTISTS AND PERFORMERS

It is sometimes difficult for schools to find skilled artists and performers—not because there is not an adequate supply of them, but because some of the most able artists and performers simply do not know how to get their foot in the door and make schools aware of them. Natalie Bergman's experience was typical. "Our group had performed regularly throughout the region and we had always been well received by the critics. So we decided we should expand our group's impact and increase our earnings by offering a multi-session performance and workshop program for local elementary schools. We spent a lot of time working on the program and we thought it was excellent. Schools should have been beating down our door, or so we thought."

But Natalie and the group found that it was tougher to drum up interest in the program than anyone had imagined. She called seven local elementary schools and described the program. In each case, she was given the cold shoulder — "Ms. Jones will call you back when she has time." (Ms. Jones never did.) Or "We don't have any money for concerts; we get people who want to play for the experience." (Yeah, thought Natalie, the experience of being a poor musician.) She wanted some glimmer of interest before she spent money on a brochure, but the responses she was getting were not encouraging.

"Thank goodness for the Bennett School. I was so discouraged when I had gotten no response after several weeks that I told my troubles to a good friend who has a child in the school. She suggested that I come to a Parent-Teacher Organization meeting and be prepared to discuss and even demonstrate some of the possible in-school activities our group could offer. It was great. Finally someone was interested. Parents and teachers were so impressed with what they saw and heard that they unanimously voted to contribute some of their program funds to support a special project. Our group was on its way."

Artists and performers often have a difficult time getting past the initial barrier to be seen, heard, or considered by school representatives. As creative as they are in their professional lives, they often lack imagination when it comes to selling themselves. Many rely on printed flyers and brochures, but these are much less effective than more informal networks of communication. They learn that the most difficult way to gain attention is to approach a school or school system cold, with no personal contacts, the way Natalie did. Personal connections, no matter how tenuous, break down the initial barrier, which is usually the most difficult hurdle.

School people can help by using their special networks of communication to promote the work of outstanding artists and performers. Not only does this help the artists but it also helps other schools design quality arts-in-education programs. Word-of-mouth networking is most effective, and artists and performers should be encouraged to ask principals and teachers to recommend them to their colleagues in other schools. Often school representatives are flattered to be asked for the help.

The process of identifying and selecting artists has already been described in detail in Chapter 2. It is obviously a crucial part of designing an arts-in-education program. The success of the program will depend in large measure on the energies, skills, and enthusiasm of the artists and performers who are chosen.

WHAT IS PREPLANNING?

Preplanning is the trouble-shooting that goes on before a contract is drawn up between the artist or performer and the school itself. If a program is limited to a single event such as a performance, preplanning can be handled over the telephone. In the case of performing groups that offer a prepackaged program, the process is simple. Space requirements, audience size limitations, additional equipment needs, and time of arrival are the standard issues that need to be checked out. On longer-term residencies, it may be necessary for artists or performers and school representatives to meet face-to-face before the contract is signed. Ultimately, time invested at this point makes the possibility of a smooth, trouble-free residency more likely.

The initial meeting sets the tone for all later relationships, so friendliness and cooperation are important. However, neither artists and performers nor school representatives should shirk from being honest and frank about their needs, their limitations, and their expectations. It is sometimes easier if everyone works from a checklist of areas to be covered, which might look something like this:

Preplanning Checklist

1. **Goals** — What are the school's priorities and goals? Is the emphasis on reading, writing, and arithmetic, or on helping children to express themselves creatively? Do the teachers have a clear idea of what artists will do in the school, and of their goals for children? Are their goals in conflict? Will the artist be used as an add-on or an extracurricular activity, or is he or she expected to be at the center of the curriculum?

2. **Teaching Philosophy** — What is the artist's approach to learning and teaching? What is the school's? Does one prefer student-directed experiences while the other relies on teacher-directed activities? What about group versus individual work? structured versus flexible activities? Teachers and artists often speak different professional languages. Do they understand

each other's jargon? If artists talk about "the power of accident" or teachers talk about "the centrality of cognitive growth," will they understand each other? It is best if everyone can speak very specifically about what they want to see happen with the students.

3. **School Experience with Arts Programs** — Do the artists and teachers have previous experiences with arts programs? Does either group feel dragooned into meeting because the assistant principal decided that it was important? Are teachers interested in talking about a ballet program because it seems noncontroversial? Or are they using dance as a way to introduce science students to abstraction in the creative process? What personal and institutional experiences do these teachers bring to their discussions? Are artists genuinely interested in the school curriculum or do they simply want to present a prepackaged program?

4. **Mechanics** — What about the mechanics of the program? Occasionally even the best programs are thwarted because not enough attention is given to school calendars, special days, overall curriculum and scheduling, and availability of space and materials. How will the artist learn if there is a snow day? How flexible are the forty-two minute periods? Whom does the artist call if he or she is sick, and when?

5. **Other Activities** — What other special programs are going on in the school? Will the artist coordinate with, or be in competition with, the regional spelling bee or the Rotary essay contest? Will the artist be working with the same students over a period of weeks, or will some students always be missing on Tuesdays, others unable to come on Fridays? Do teachers want artists to dovetail their work with ongoing classroom activities and do teachers have ideas about how to make collaboration a reality?

6. **Liaison** — What will happen to the program if the arts-in-education contact person leaves the school? Who will take over? How much does this person know about the program?

7. **Space** — What space will be available? If the artist is going to be in residence, where will he or she be working? One painter with lots of experience working in schools writes:

> I just can't say enough about how important space is to the success of a residency. I've been in janitor's closets, basement rooms with no natural light, and in a glassed-in office — which was terrible (like being in a fish bowl). You have to insist on a good studio space or your whole residency will be impossible. When I first started, I tried to be a nice, accommodating person and take whatever they offered, but it backfired every time. If the space wasn't right, I couldn't work and was miserable the whole time. It's important to be flexible, but you really should make your needs known right at the beginning and don't settle for less-than-optimum studio conditions. That's one of

the keys to a good residency. At least that's the way it is for visual artists. And you *must* have running water in the studio. None of this going down the hall to wash the brushes. It just doesn't work.

At the end of a preplanning session, artists, teachers, and others involved should ask themselves how they feel about the proposed activities. Assuming no contract has been signed and no formal commitment has been made to the school, there is still time to withdraw. If artists and teachers disagree on major issues, if the situation "feels wrong," both sides have the opportunity to back out. A difficult or antagonistic residency will make life miserable for everyone and will also influence how the school feels about the arts. Sometimes the chemistry just isn't right; artists and teachers should not feel that they have to force it.

WHAT ARE THE NEXT STEPS?

Assuming that both sides feel positively about continuing, several additional administrative details must be attended to:

1. **Sign a contract.** A contract is a legal agreement between two parties. To be effective, contracts should be detailed and specific. A contract between artists or performers at a school should include:

—name, address, telephone number, and Social Security number of artist or performer (In the case of a group, no Social Security number is necessary, but it is helpful to include both the name of the contact person and information on both the artistic director and the manager.)

—name, address, and telephone number of school and the individual who will serve as the primary school contact

—schedule for the program (hours, days, weeks)

—number and characteristics of the students to be served

—description of the space the artists or performers will have available

—list of supplies and equipment the school will provide and list of supplies and equipment the artist will be expected to contribute or purchase.

—description of artist's responsibilities, including an outline of activities with the students and an acknowledgment of responsibility for preparing a final report (if appropriate)

—payment for the artist (amount, procedures, schedule)

—benefits (compensations for sick days or snow days?)

—copyright and ownership of materials

—conditions for termination of the contract, by artist or by the school

The function of a contract is often misunderstood. Many people feel that it is a legal document that allows one party to sue if the other does not live up to its side of the agreement. As a result, some artists resist contracts. They know that they would never have any intention or financial wherewithal to embark on a lawsuit, so they reason that it is not worth spending a lot of time on a contract that could give the school legal grounds to sue them over some technicality.

This interpretation represents a fundamental misunderstanding of the main function of a contract. A contract simply spells out, in writing, what each side expects from the other. In going through the discipline of writing things out, many confusions and misconceptions can be straightened out before they become problems. By having a written document to refer to, the artist and school avoid having both sides recollect an oral agreement differently six months after it was made. Contracts for arts programs almost never end up in the hands of lawyers and courts — litigation is too expensive and the dollars involved are too small. But carefully crafted contracts help avoid headaches and misunderstandings.

2. **Include the budget.** The financial details of the program must be clear to all concerned and should be described in the contract. Often this is very simple: "Artist fee for a one-hour workshop with ten students is..." Sometimes, however, it is necessary to be detailed and complex, giving the costs for supplies, transportation, even phone, secretarial, and copying costs. The longer and more flexible the program, the more complex the budget. It is impossible to prepare a realistic budget until an artists has talked with the school about expectations, goals, and objectives of the program. For example, when cellist Natalie Bergman sat down to discuss budgets, she learned that the school expected the string quartet to perform in the evening for students and parents as a kick-off to the special residency program. While she agreed that this was a wonderful idea, she had to explain that the quartet would need some remuneration and that would mean amending the budget she had first proposed.

Level-headed and direct budget discussions ensure that the school knows exactly what it is getting and how much it will cost. Artists and performers are similarly protected from unrealistic (and uncompensated) demands for additional services at a later date. Neither side likes to feel taken advantage of. Artists are professionals and must be compensated; by the same token, the school needs to know exactly what it is buying.

A clearly delineated budget also gives artists and schools a series of milestones against which to measure the program. If an artist finds it necessary to buy more paint halfway through the residency because the students are interested in preparing a larger mural than had been planned, this gives everyone a chance to review the progress of the residency relative to the original objectives and expectations. It may turn out that money can be taken from some other part of the budget to pay for the paint, or that additional funds are offered by parents or the school because of the success of the residency. Artists should try to avoid paying for unforeseen expenses out of their own pockets. While they often find it to be less hassle, it is also unfair and unprofessional; artists should not be subsidizing their own residencies.

What should be included in a budget? The following checklist seems to cover most items:

Budget Checklist

a. **Artist's Compensation** — Will the artist be paid by the day? by the hour? for a fixed fee for the entire job? Will there be compensation for planning time? or for directing after-school workshops for teachers?

b. **Supplies** — Will these be for the artist or just for the students? Will the artist be expected to pay first and be reimbursed later, or can some funds be advanced? Can the school buy supplies at a discounted rate?

c. **Publicity** — Who will pay for the photographer to cover the opening of the students' exhibit? Who will type the press releases or the notices sent home to parents? Who will buy after-performance refreshments?

d. **Evaluation** — Will there be an outside evaluator? Is it required by the people who are paying for your program? If so, how will the evaluator be paid?

e. **Documentation** — Does the poet-in-residence want to produce a book of poetry written by her students? Does the visual artist want to produce a video-tape of his studio sessions? Do the performers think an audio-tape of the concert would be beneficial? If so, be sure to budget appropriately.

f. **Display Materials** — How will student art work be matted and hung? Will the school assume the cost? Will students be expected to foot the bill?

g. **Travel** — If the artist does not live in the community where the school is located, how will he or she get to the school? What if the artist wants to take the students on a field trip to a museum or to a forest or to a city street? If the artist is expected to bring heavy equipment, who will pay for the van that must be rented to bring the equipment to the school?

h. **Insurance** — If equipment, materials, or artwork is left at the school, is special insurance needed? Does the school need extra insurance?

i. **Teacher Overtime** — If you want artists to work with teachers after school, does the teachers' union contract require that they be paid overtime?

j. **Unanticipated Expenses** — Always leave something in the budget for contingencies.

Some of these costs can be absorbed by the school and will not involve the expenditure of extra cash, but it always helps to write down all expenses and talk about where the money will come from. It is also valuable for everyone to know the full cost of a residency, even if many of the expenses turn out to be of the "in-kind" or donated variety. Talking through the program in budget terms will raise questions like, "Does the school secretary have time to type the press releases? If not, who will do it?" "Will the custodian stay after school for the special reception for parents and the school committee?"

In the course of the budget and contract negotiations, artists and performers should be told how they will be paid. Do they have to submit timesheets or an invoice, or does the school have to prepare a purchase order for their services? Will they be paid on the first or last day of the project? or six months later? Schools are bureaucracies that have their own schedules for processing payments. As a result artists and performers may have to wait days, weeks, even months to get paid. Many who have counted on a payment to cover their rent on the first of the month have found themselves pleading unsuccessfully with a school fiscal officer to speed up the check processing in the middle of the month. It is only fair play to tell artists and performers early in the discussions what the payment procedure will be.

If the project is supported by grant funds, it should be made clear who is the "fiscal agent," that is, who will actually receive and be handling the money. Will it be the school? the city? a local arts council? Find out who has responsibility for filling out forms, writing reports or saving financial documentation after the program is over. If equipment is to be purchased with grant funds, find out who will own the equipment after the residency is over.

Some artists have learned the hard way that the equipment is not simply the noncash portion of their fee:

> Michael Brown, a photographer who spent four months in a middle school, kept no records, but did keep an enlarger that he was told was the noncash portion of his fee. Three years after his residency was over, the granting state agency audited the school he had worked in. In the course of the audit, Michael was asked to come to the school and bring with him the receipts documenting the purchases of darkroom supplies and cameras. "And," the auditors wanted to know, "where is that special enlarger that you bought with state funds? The school has been searching for it but has been unable to find it."

3. **Prepare a schedule.** Once a contract has been signed and the details of the budget worked out, there is one more important document to prepare — the schedule. In addition to the obvious blocks of time when the artists will be in school working with students, there may be other time slots

for regular planning meetings or evaluation sessions with the school staff. Artists and teachers must work out these meeting schedules. Early mornings might be the traditional time for teachers to gather and discuss the week's or day's schedule, while artists may prefer to hold teacher workshops after school or on the weekends. Each may have to compromise.

For performers, set-up time may be important, particularly where scenery, costumes, and large instruments are involved. Warm-up time may also be required. The school should know when performers will arrive and what assistance they will need. If several performance sites are involved, the coordinator should provide the performers with a master schedule, a map, and a list of school contacts for each site (with school and home phone numbers in case of emergency).

4. **Exchange phone numbers.** Artists and performers should be sure to find out how they can reach teachers or school contacts on short notice. If an artist has an emergency over the weekend that will keep him out of school the following Monday, can the school be notified of this fact over a weekend? Who is notified in case of illness? By the same token, artists should not forget to give the school their home number and other phone numbers where it is likely they can be reached. One artist gave the school her own number, but did not give the number of her sister with whom she was planning to live for the month of February. On the below-zero day that the school's furnace stopped working, no one was able to reach her to say, "don't bother coming to school." And her sister lived in a town many miles from the school!

5. **Establish an in-school coordinator.** In the course of the planning sessions with teachers and school staff, an artist meets and talks with many people. It is important that one person is designated as the coordinator, as the person responsible for helping make the program run smoothly. It should be someone who has been in the school long enough to know how to get things done — how to find an extra $10 to pay for refreshments for the reception, how to convince the superintendent to attend a performance, how to smooth over tense situations. An energetic and helpful person outside the school, like an enthusiastic parent or a local arts council representative, may make a good coordinator for short-term programs like performances.

For longer-term residencies, however, the program will be more successful if the coordinator is based in the school. There are always unanticipated problems, and it is good to have an on-site person with authority who can help out.

When more than one site is used for a series of in-school events, each site should have a contact person. At the very least this person should be at the school to greet artists or performers when they arrive for the first time, make introductions, act as a guide, and find out what the artist needs.

WHAT ABOUT THE PROGRAM ITSELF?

Artists and school representatives often have recurring nightmares about arts-in-education programs. They worry that if things can go wrong, they will go wrong. Such worrying is normal and a few words about the most common nightmares may be helpful.

Nightmare No. 1 — The Program Is Lousy

If the planning has been comprehensive, both artist and school should be looking forward to a wonderful program, a swirl of activity and excitement that energizes children and teachers alike. But what if things do not work out that way? What if the enthusiasm that everyone expected to see on the children's faces as they participated in the magic of creating new art or mastering the intricacies of performance, simply do not occur? It is absolutely essential at this point NOT TO PANIC. What is occurring is normal. It takes time and practice to perfect arts-in-education programs. It is important for everyone to be patient and not to be completely discouraged.

What steps can be taken? First, everyone involved should take a little time to stand back and observe the program from a distance. Are people's expectations being met? What do people say informally at lunch or after school? Are things really as bad as they seem? Take some positive steps to discover what is working well. What makes some activities work better than others? What small changes can be made to minimize the negative and accentuate the positive? Try not to be a perfectionist. Effective arts-in-education programs are built by people who work persistently to improve but who can tolerate situations that are less than ideal.

Do not misread shyness or nervousness for lack of enthusiasm and support. Many students and teachers are nervous about participating in a new activity, but this does not necessarily mean a lack of interest. Artists and performers may be very nervous as they present activities for the first time but this does not mean a lack of enthusiasm. Misreading cues was the mistake of Lisette, a dancer, who was devastated to find that one second-grade teacher, very enthusiastic during planning meetings, never followed through with activities in her classrooms. Lisette stewed over the situation for awhile, then decided to invite the teacher out for a cup of coffee before school. Over coffee, she learned that this teacher had had an up-setting experience with her own dance teacher while in high school. The high school teacher had told her that she had little dance ability and should attempt only simple steps. Since then, although she enjoyed dance, she was loath to try improvisation, especially in front of an audience, even her classroom students. After this discussion, Lisette invited the teacher to participate in the improvisational activities she was doing with the students.

And in a few weeks the teacher suggested ideas that she and Lisette could work on together with the second-grade students. A year later, dance activities were a regular part of her classroom activities.

Nightmare No. 2 — "My Studio and Supplies Are Gone"

Many artists worry that on some Monday they will return to the school and find that someone has taken all of their supplies or has converted their studio into a classroom with rows of desks. Performers worry that their scenery will be carted off to the dump or that the assembly room will be unavailable for the rehearsal, even though it was promised. In a school where everyone, from the custodian to the principal, knows why artists and performers are there and what they are doing and will be doing, this nightmare is less likely to become reality. Once again, involving as many people as possible and making a point of keeping everyone up-to-date on the activities, is a special form of insurance.

In addition, putting all agreements in writing makes everyone less likely to forget what was promised. Artists can be encouraged to draw up a weekly plan that they circulate to the school community four or five days before the week is to begin. Not only is a written plan a good way to trouble-shoot potential problems, but it also offers a chance to express needs and worries in a humorous way — "Two chocolate chip cookies to anyone who lets us have an extra half hour in the assembly room next week." "Please don't borrow my paints over the weekend — we all want to do our nails on Monday!"

Nightmare No. 3 — No One Will Bend

Very few arts programs follow initial plans and outlines to the letter. New ideas emerge, unexpected pockets of energy are found, unanticipated constraints appear. While artists are often asked to be flexible enough to roll with the punches or ride the tide of enthusiasm, they sometimes think that the school is far less flexible. But this perception is often uninformed by the larger picture of the complexity of schools as institutions and the needs of those who work in them. Just as an artist might be adamant about the size and convenience of her studio space, preserving the schedule might be "the bottom line" for an assistant principal. One artist put it this way:

> It used to frustrate me a lot when I would go into schools because everything seems so rigid. Schedules, for example. If you asked to change the schedule, to move a class up or something, everybody would get irritable. Slowly I learned how much that goes on in schools is the responsibility of specialists — the speech teacher who sees two or three kids from the fourth grade between 11:45 and lunch, the Title I tutor who works with the bottom math group

sandwiched in between recess and the start of the science lesson. Every spare moment is used and the schedule is a finely tuned instrument that allows many specialists access to the children who need their services. A principal pointed out to me once that asking to move my core group back a half hour one day influenced seven different teachers in one way or other. It really was true. The schedule is complex in a school that offers lots of opportunities for kids and lots of services for their special problems and needs. It sure makes my life seem simple and even sparse (a necessity for me to accomplish anything). When I'm working in a school, I see how different my personal sense of time is. It's hard not to feel that schools are rigid and inflexible. It's hard not to be judgmental about that.

Since flexibility on everyone's part is often a key element of a successful program, an important role that the coordinator can play is mediating between artists and school people, encouraging both sides to bend.

Public Information or How to Avoid the "Best Kept Secret" Phenomenon

There are many wonderful arts-in-education programs in schools. But too often not enough people know about them. They are victims of what is known as the "best kept secret" phenomenon. Consider the plight of the African dance program that took place some years ago in a Massachusetts school. Teachers and students alike loved the dancers and the work they did over a six-week period. As follow-up to the residency, a number of students pursued African dance in private classes. Everyone was looking forward to an expanded residency the following year. During the summer, however, the school learned that it would not receive continued funding for the program. A group of parents and teachers desperately approached local givers and the school committee for new funds. They learned that the program they had loved was unknown to the broader community. No one had heard about it or remembered that it had happened. There were no newspaper articles to point to, no video-tapes, and no photographs. Even the students who had been most enthusiastic were dispersed for the summer and unavailable to talk about their personal experiences. No one was willing to put money into the second year of the program.

Had this school engaged in a public information campaign during the residency, the story might have had a different and happier ending. Public information should be a vital piece in the life of any arts-in-education program. For most people in the broader community, the program will not exist until it has been written about in a newspaper, has been filmed and shown on television, or has been the subject of a public service announcement on the radio. Public information increases support for any program, it involves more people in the activities, and it introduces the community to

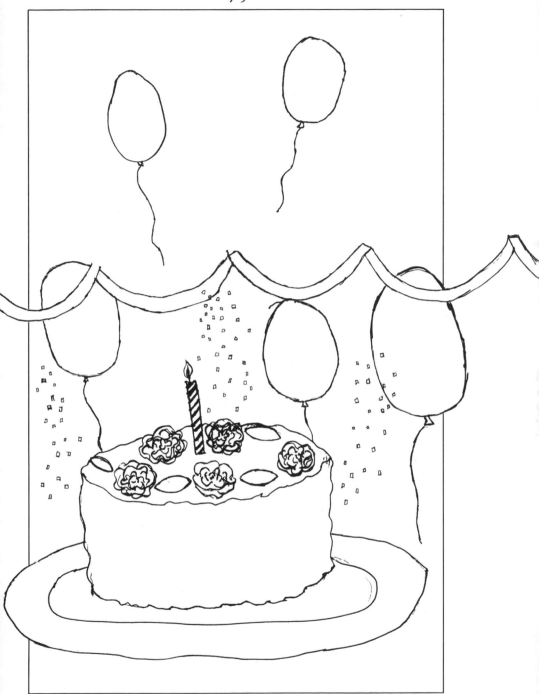

the uniqueness of the work. The responsibilities of carrying out a public information campaign should be taken seriously and incorporated into program plans from day one.

Arts programs that develop a public information plan with a specific timeline are a step ahead of those in which publicity is done in an ad hoc manner. Teachers in some Boston schools have found the schedule in Figure 4.1 useful in structuring their public information plans.

Figure 4.1.
A Public Information Schedule

	Oct.	Nov.	Dec.	Jan.	Feb.	Mar.	Apr.	May	June
Article in School Newspaper									
Article in Local Community Paper									
Article in Periodical									
Presentation to:_____									
Presentation to:_____									
TV Talk Show									
Radio Talk Show									
Faculty Meeting									
Parents Involvement (at least twice) 1. _____ 2. _____									
Other (Please specify)									

The key to a successful public information campaign is to send out information through pre-existing networks and to use contacts that have already been developed, beginning in the school or district. Is there a school newsletter that goes to parents? Who writes it? How do teachers find out about activities in other schools in the district? Does the superintendent have a regular way of communicating with the general public, or with the school committee or board of education? If broader publicity is desired for the program—because it is an important model or attempts something new—someone might write an article for a professional journal. Such coverage not only has obvious public relations value but also lends an air of legitimacy to the entire program.

No matter what form of public information is used, the following guidelines can make the job easier:

1. Maintain a list of local newspapers, public bulletin boards, radio and television stations that sponsor public service announcements. Know their deadlines for submitting news items, calendar announcements, and press releases. Send in materials well in advance of the date they need to be published or announced. Follow up your correspondence with phone calls.

2. Target each information piece at a particular audience and make its purpose clear.

3. Invite members of the local media to classes, performances, and events in order to inform them of your program. Present the events to the media as if they are public events that should be covered.

4. Acknowledge funding sources in publicity whenever possible.

5. Keep a record of successful public information efforts. This record of names and resources will be invaluable in public relations strategy.

6. Ask people who know about the program how they learned about it. Continue providing information to these sources.

7. Word-of-mouth communication is often underestimated and underused. It is still the primary source of information, particularly for people who work in schools. Everyone in the immediate school community should be well informed about the project and encouraged to share information with others.

The "Celebration"

As a clincher to the publicity campaign and as an acknowledgement of the completion of a wonderful project, nothing can beat a celebration. This is a chance to share with a greater public what has happened in a residency and to build support for continuing the project. Invite local legislators, school committee members, town council members, local educators, and the media. Well-planned and well-publicized events draw together the crucial mix of people necessary to push for continuation of the program in the future.

Residency celebrations can take many forms including arts festivals, exhibits, performances of students' and artists' work, unveilings, and dedications. The more creative the celebration, the more impact it will have. The following is a good example:

> During a program exploring local folklore, students from a school in Little Compton, Rhode Island, constructed life-sized scarecrows. These soft sculptures, along with other residency products, were displayed in the school library. On the day of the program's celebration, a small band assembled, and students, scarecrows, and observers paraded through the town commons. At the end of the procession, the scarecrows were planted in a local field. A bonfire was lit and a community picnic held that afternoon.

HOW IMPORTANT IS DOCUMENTATION?

Disseminating public information is a mechanism for sharing the arts-in-education experience with the community at large. Program participants and others closely involved need a more detailed record of a project. Internal documentation records for participants the development of a program. It also provides an excellent vehicle for communicating to others what the program really does for participants.

Documenting the program is useful for:
— displaying skills learned by participants;
— training new participants;
— illustrating the program to interested supporters;
— securing current or future funding;
— reporting back to grantors.

Documenting the teacher-training portions of residencies can provide irreplaceable background materials and tools for teachers carrying out activities after the artist has left. Such information is also useful for disseminating a project through a school system. Principals, superintendents, and other administrators can use documentary material to support their efforts toward continuing or expanding a program.

Before documenting begins, determine exactly why it is needed and who the audience(s) will be. Select a medium that will best capture the essence of the program and satisfy the target audience. Also consider whether or not the medium will interfere with the program. Will it disturb people to be filmed while they are working?

Figure 4.2.

Ways to Document Your Arts Program

Visual: includes photographs, slides	*Considerations:* Do you need a photographer? Will you use black and white or color? Photographs or slides? Is a darkroom available or will work be sent to a lab?
Printed: includes newsletters, brochures	*Considerations:* Who will be the chief editor? Will someone else write copy? Will photographs be included? Will the materials be typeset?
Audiovisual: includes slide tapes, video-tapes, audio-tapes, films	*Considerations:* Will an audiotape accompany slides? Will tape and slides be synchronized? What are the rental costs of equipment? Is quality reel-to-reel or cassette tape equipment available? Will someone on staff be able to edit the tapes or will a technician be needed? Does a staff person know how to operate the equipment?
Products: includes materials completed by participants, poetry, games & toys, books, crafts, journals, performances	*Considerations:* What is the best method of organizing and displaying these products? Will participants be willing and prepared to perform at the end? Is there performance space available? Will excerpts from journals or poetry be printed for distribution? Do participants want to keep their final products?

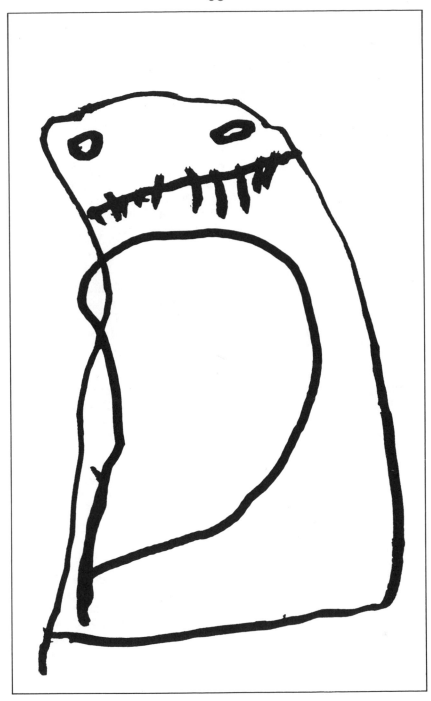

There are many different media for documentation, but each raises different questions. See Figure 4.2 (page 79) for specific guidelines.

Documentation should be subject to the same care and planning as other aspects of the program and decisions about how it should be accomplished should be made during the planning stage. Draft a timeline for documentation and, depending on the budget, decide whether to document throughout the program or only at specific stages. Involve project participants, parents, and staff in the documentation process. Artists should think about whether it might be possible to incorporate the documentation process into their projects. Shooting a film, producing a book, creating a slide show, or making an audio-tape are all examples of documentation that can serve the residency as well.

IS IT NECESSARY TO DO AN EVALUATION?

"If there is anything that can throw cold water over my work in schools, it is an evaluation," says one artisan with much arts-in-education experience. "The very word conjures up images in my mind of failure. I will be evaluated and I will not make the grade. I have found that teachers also do not exactly welcome the idea of an evaluation. They tell me that they are evaluated all the time and that things like their tenure decisions and salaries depend to an extent on the results. If there is anything that seems to bring artists and teachers together, it is the negative reaction to an evaluation."

The response of this craftsperson to an evaluation of his residency is not untypical. Few people feel totally comfortable with the idea of an evaluation of their program partly because the results may reflect badly on them as professionals. But evaluations *are* important. They can help in improving the quality of an arts-in-education program by identifying both its most successful and least successful elements. They can help make a case for continuation of a program by identifying its effects on those being served. Just as important, evaluations can serve as a kind of "certificate of accountability" — that is, they can state quite clearly to friend and foe alike that the money expended on the program had a definite and specific impact and that the program was responsibly administered.

There are two kinds of evaluation. The first kind, *program evaluation*, *evaluates the quality of the program by looking at how it was carried out*. The focus is on the activities, the personnel, the administrative details, and the funding. The second kind of evaluation focuses less on the program and instead *evaluates its effects*. It looks at a specific group — children, for example — and measures how their lives were changed as a result of the residency. An extensive evaluation combines both types.

Program Evaluation

If a school with an ongoing arts-in-education program wants to refine and improve it, an evaluation will establish which aspects of the program can be strengthened. There are several points to consider as the evaluation is planned:

1. Find out what specific things should be evaluated before designing the evaluation. There is no such thing as a *standard* evaluation form that will work in all cases. The best evaluations are custom designed to the situation.

2. Ask focused questions. The information that comes from an evaluation is only as good as the questions asked. Questions like "Was the program a success?" are too vague and open ended. More focused questions might be: "What were the three activities that children were most enthusiastic about?" "Do you feel that there is an ideal length of time that should be blocked out for most of the residency activities? If so, how long should it be?" "Was the budget adequate? If not, where would you use additional funds?" "Do you feel that the contact time between artist and teachers was adequate? If not, how might you restructure the residency to allow for more contact time with teachers?"

3. Look for multiple points of view. You will probably not be able to go into depth with everyone involved in the program, so get representatives from a variety of groups — teachers who worked with the artists, teachers who did not work with the artists, administrators, parents, students, custodial staff, and artists and performers. Getting multiple points of view assures greater objectivity.

4. Keep things *simple*. No one wants to be burdened with a lot of paperwork. Take the time to design a questionnaire that asks only as many questions as you feel are absolutely necessary. Since people's oral answers to questions tend to be more complete than their written ones, consider talking to people instead of surveying them through a questionnaire. Keep to a standardized set of questions so that you can compare and contrast the answers from various people to the same question.

5. *Use* the results. All too often, much time is spent on an evaluation that is ignored. If you do a serious program evaluation, its results should serve you well as you design your programs for the future.

Evaluating Program Effects

A school board, a group of parents, or a funding source often wants to know what *effects* an arts-in-education program has had on students. There are two kinds of effects that can be measured: the effect of the program on children's understanding or enjoyment of the art; and the effects of the arts program on some other aspect of the students' school activities such as reading, science, mathematics, or even school attendance. The desire to produce extravagant claims in the second area often leads to trouble. While it is probably true that over the long haul a school with a rich arts program will have better school attendance or higher reading scores than a school that does not, it is virtually impossible to document such an effect. The difficulty of proving the effects is compounded by the expense of designing reliable, vertifiable tests and administering them. In evaluating program effects, consider several things:

1. Who is the evaluation for? Is it for the funders? the school board? parents? What would representatives of these groups consider an adequate indication of success?

2. Try to evaluate success in the context of the arts themselves, not in terms of some other area of the curriculum. It is much easier to demonstrate the impact of a poetry residency on students' ability to write stories and verse, for example, than it is to show its impact on mathematics skills or student self-image.

3. While professional evaluators tend to want to set quantifiable objectives, try to avoid a statistical evaluation. The arts lend themselves more readily to a descriptive approach, and no good statistical measures of artistic or affective growth have yet been designed. Stay away from standardized tests, particularly those that measure unreleated activities like reading and mathematics skills. Though there may be great pressure to try to demonstrate that exposure to the arts increases reading test scores, do not bow to it. In the end, you will not be able to rest your claims on student performance on such tests.

4. If you feel uncertain, hire a professional to help you design your evaluation and perhaps even carry it out for you. The evaluator can help you think through what are reasonable indications of program success and how to look for them.

5. Again, keep things simple. As in all evaluation, the more complicated the design, the more difficult (and expensive) it is to carry out.

Finally, look on evaluation less as a burden and more as an opportunity. There is hardly anyone who would not rather spend the time and money reserved for evaluation on the program itself. But evaluation ultimately can and should lead to better programs. As one foundation executive in New England put it:

> The arts-in-education people have been making extravagant claims about their programs for years. My hunch is that by making those claims they have been able to avoid looking squarely at the question of why the programs are important and how they can

be made better. Our foundation is looking for accountability — we need to know that the money is spent prudently and wisely. But beyond that we want there to be a clearer statement of purpose and a strategy that will lead to better programs in the future. We think evaluations will help.

How about Next Year?

"No matter how well an arts program is going, I always remind myself that the arts-in-education field is tenuous at best and that I had better be thinking about whether or not we can have a similar program next year." These are the words of a teacher at the Bennett School who has learned that it is dangerous to take things for granted. "I have seen so many successful programs that are here today and gone tomorrow. Often artists could help more. In addition to the wonderful activites they offer to kids, they could try to make additional connections with teachers and parents. They should not forget that if teachers and parents fight hard for a program, there is a good chance they will get it."

This teacher suggests several specific ways artists can help:

1. Always support the classroom teacher in front of parents, children, and colleagues. If teachers believe that an artist is with them, instead of in competition, they will be more likely to advocate for his or her return.

2. Encourage teachers who are already making efforts to use the arts in their classrooms. Praise them and include them in activities.

3. Ask teachers about their curriculum plans and bring in activities that support their plans. Teach by example rather than by imposing ideas.

4. Share students' work with the rest of the school.

5. Even if artists are working primarily with a small group of students and one or two teachers, they should attempt to include some activities with a large number of students and other teachers.

6. Spend time with the principal and arts specialists. Let them know what is going on and let them share in the process of the residency.

7. Never underestimate the power of parents. Make it a point to invite them to events. Solicit their support in having the program continue.

There are other things everyone involved in the arts program should do to attempt to get the arts permanently institutionalized in the school:

1. Develop a multi-year plan to phase the arts activities into the regular school program. While financial support from the community is

important, in the long run the project should be taken over by the school or school district.

2. Develop a long-term fund-raising plan that incorporates many of the ideas contained in the following chapter on fund raising.

3. Maintain a file of program information, including an abstract describing the program, the history of its development, and evaluations. Use the documentary products to supplement this file.

4. Explore and develop local networks for supporting the project. At the school level, speak regularly with the superintendent, curriculum officials, and other administrators. Suggest the formation of a Council or Task Force within the school system that has arts education as its primary agenda.

5. Invite community leaders, legislators, and other potential supporters to program events. Find out what individuals, organizations, and governmental units should be receiving program information and put them on the mailing list.

6. Bring together artists, performers, and administrative staff from arts organizations to discuss collaborative programming possibilities with school representatives. Demonstrate the cost effectiveness of such plans and show how they will contribute to the curriculum of the school.

7. Make contact with your state arts agency and your local arts council. If they know about what you are doing, they can often be helpful in a variety of ways.

"Sure, it's a battle," says painter Sylvan Smith. "I learned long ago that the arts program is not as important as the football program in the lives of most schools. But I also learned something else. There are a lot of people in the school who care deeply and are willing to stick their necks out for us. But they need us to help. The survival of the arts program is not just their problem. It is everyone's problem. If there is no arts program, I don't eat. So I have learned how to help in a variety of ways to make sure that people want me back and want the arts to continue. It is a funny thing. As you find yourself working with teachers, parents, and kids toward the same goal, suddenly you forget that 'we / they' nonsense. And from that day on, most of the big problems seem to disappear."

Chapter 4
Planning the Contents of an Artist's Visit

by Dennie Palmer Wolf

"Phew, that's nearly over," you think, as you drive away from the last meeting about a year's worth of residencies and performances in the junior-high. "Now that the dollars and the days are nailed down, all that's left is to make sure the kids and the artists turn up in the same place at the same time."

Well, not quite. Still ahead is one of the most important steps in bringing artists into schools — the "what" of arts programs. If you have funds, approval, dates, and artists, you have settled the "how" and the "who" of your program. But the "what" still hangs fire — *What* are the artists going to do? *What* are kids going to get out of it? *What* can teachers expect?

"Now wait a minute," you say to yourself. "I agreed to drum up support for the program and make the arrangements. But I am not an artist or program designer. Even if I do have ideas, I don't know that they are good or workable. Besides, if I step in, won't artists feel I'm meddling…"

In many instances, either the artist, the school, the teachers or you, as the advocate or sponsor for an arts-in-education program, is new to the idea of visits or residencies by outside artists. The process of planning what will happen is an excellent way to learn about the basic ingredients, the options, the pitfalls, and the potential of having or being an artist in the schools. Anyone who is new to the process will be saved mistakes and guaranteed more exciting results if they put time into planning the contents or curriculum of upcoming artistic events or residencies. There certainly are artists, teachers, and parents who are wise in the ways of bringing arts experiences into classrooms and assembly halls. But even where the partners are experienced, the process of bringing artists into schools is greatly strengthened and smoothed when there is a groundplan that covers more than dates, fees, and audience sizes. Not planning the "curriculum" of a residency is something like buying the building supplies for an entire house, then "saving" time and money by not bothering with blueprints.

Consider the differences between these two visits by visual artists to middle-school classrooms in the same community:

At the Manter school, the science, reading, and art teachers had worked with the artist ahead of time and had agreed that they all wanted to collaborate on an illustration project. Ahead of time, the teachers had asked children to make folders of their own drawings. They had collected drawings from other children, made a chronological display, talked about the way that people develop drawing skills, and also discussed their own concerns about being able to "draw things the way that they really look." In addition, the librarian showed them books with a wide range of illustrations, some quite fanciful and abstract. At the same time, children wrote stories they wanted to illustrate. When the artist arrived, children were overflowing with ideas. The artist showed children how to communicate feeling and mood and worked with them on developing a personal style of drawing. During her stay, the artist also worked on a book of poems written by one of her friends. The residency ended with the illustrated books being read aloud and shown to other classrooms, then displayed along with the artist's work in the front hall of the school. Following the residency, two school parents, one who had worked for a newspaper and one who was a writer, came and talked with classes about what pictures add to print. Even several months after the residency, the librarian would share new illustrated books with children who had been involved in the original activity.

At the Currier School, the same artist arrived on the first day of the residency and found a group of fifth graders who had just learned that she was coming. For the first several weeks, she and the students struggled with their prejudices about visual art —

"As far as they were concerned, you either had to be batiking t-shirts or making photographic-looking horses or self-portraits. So the first couple of weeks, they mostly filled wastebaskets with false starts. I think I was frustrated. I had planned to pack the first year of art school into ten-year-olds in three weeks. In order to have something that looked good, we spent the whole last week framing and displaying some sketches that I ended up practically telling kids how to do."

Securing the funding, an artist, and a date to begin does not ensure an arts-in-education program that will effectively teach and excite children about the arts. That takes thinking and planning. This chapter discusses how to plan either a single event or a residency so that it reaches and affects its audience.

"WE CAN SCHEDULE THE QUARTET IN MUSIC PERIOD, CAN'T WE?"

Sometimes there is the superstition that an arts-in-education program can replace the activities of art and music teachers or that such a program relieves classroom teachers of the responsibility of including the arts in the basic curriculum. In hard financial times or in communities where there is doubt about the importance of artistic learning, this can lead to dire consequences: cutting the salaries for art and music specialists, renigging on funding for art supplies, or turning studios into classrooms.

However, no arts-in-education program can flourish without basic resources. The most critical of these resources are: children who are excited by artistic learning; teachers who sustain that learning between performances or residencies, parents who think of the arts as vital, and decent supplies, space, and time. A print-maker, back from a residency in which he was the "replacement" for a full-time art teacher illustrates this point:

> No matter how much you care, if you come into a climate where people think they can get a year of art for your six-weeks fee, there is no way kids don't end up being cheated. You don't have a clue about what they've done or can do. You have to feel your way until you know their skills. By the time you're good, you're gone. There is no way to leave a note for the painter who is coming three months later. She's going to have to start from ground zero, too.

Imagine if we tried to teach reading just by hiring specialists to come in for residencies once or even ten times a year. Imagine how well children would read, if between times, there were no incentives to exercise their skills, no adults to encourage or instruct them, and no supply of books with handsome illustrations or mysterious titles to entice them. Imagine if we taught science by hiring skilled chemists and physicists to perform lecture demonstrations—who would ensure that the basic concepts were used and explored afterwards? Who would see that children had really grasped the techniques and ideas that were discussed? Similarly, while arts-in-education programs can enrich any arts curriculum, they are no substitute for the ongoing teaching and nurturing of artistic skills.

EXPOSURE OR IMMERSION: HOW MUCH ART FOR HOW MANY CHILDREN?

One of the thorniest issues that you will face is how to make the best use of funding, teachers, volunteers, and other resources. Suppose you have five hundred dollars to spend. Do you arrange for a full-scale production of *Our Town* that everyone can attend and enjoy, or do you hire an individual actor to come to the school throughout the year to work with small groups of children? The decision is difficult because it raises not one, but two, tough questions. The first question concerns learning: What are the effects of different kinds of arts programming on children's interest in and understanding of the arts?

There is little or no research to rely on, but experienced teachers and parents suggest that "lights, costumes, scenery, and never-to-be-forgotten" performances are an excellent way to initiate, punctuate, or summarize ongoing artistic learning. However, without the support of classroom activity, preparation by art and music teachers, or artists' visits to classrooms, the excitement generated by a large-scale arts event fails to send down roots. The repeated chance to work on an artistic skill, just like the repeated chance to learn to read or speak a foreign language, ensures more lasting, deeper learning. As an experienced composer put it, "Compare what it's like to hear a piece for the first time to what it's like when you are listening for the third or the tenth time. Each time you hear that music again, it's like you hear deeper, you catch layers you were deaf to before." For children who may be learning about art for the very first time, a single performance may be only enough exposure to learn what to do about feeling restless, about having a wandering imagination, or about the friend who is poking you while you try to listen. It takes many encounters to be able to listen or see aesthetically.

But providing children with the chance to immerse themselves in artistic learning, even if it is just for several weeks, is costly. Providing each child with the chance to work repeatedly with an artist often bears a larger price tag than even a series of large-scale events. Therefore, immersion programs often raise the question: If resources are limited, which children ought to have the chance to learn about the arts? Should it be the youngest ones who are still wide open to learning, the oldest ones who can sit still and be thoughtful, the learning-disabled ones who might benefit tremendously from a different sensory experience, or the gifted and talented? This particular issue is hard to resolve because it raises questions of values. In practice, many schools resolve the question by dividing their resources, allocating a portion to a series of exposure programs that offer everyone a chance to attend and the remaining portion to longer-term projects. Frequently, principals invite interested teachers or teaching teams to apply annually or establish procedures for making certain that different classes each have a chance to use school resources to provide special art experiences.

When bringing artists and performers into schools, remember that something is usually (though not always) better than nothing. If your resources only permit you one exposure per child, this may be a good starting point if everyone involved joins in planning how to extend the effects of the brief program. (The concluding sections of this chapter gives suggestions about how to accomplish this).

Remember, though, that the long-term benefits of arts programs are usually only possible with repeated exposure or immersion in the arts. It may be convenient to think of it in this way:

EXPOSURE = SPARK

IMMERSION = STAYING POWER

"IT'S GOTTA HAVE ART"

You can use a pen to pry the lid off a paint can, but you get much more out of the pen when you use it to draw or write. Similarly, you can use a dancer to offer an alternative to gym class, but the results are much greater when dancers teach the art of dancing rather than jumping jacks. If you are putting the time and effort into having a special arts program, consider making it something more than an alternative way of teaching school subjects. In other words, see that the program provides *artistic* experience. This is a tricky but vital distinction. It has to do with whether the experience focuses on aesthetic activity or whether it simply uses the tools and

contents of the arts to babysit, entertain, or teach academic skills. Two examples of music materials illustrate this difference:

> In one residency, a musician was working with Latin-American folk music. He taught children the names of all the novel instruments he used. He also taught them the names of the different rhythms like "samba," "rumba," etc. He performed a concert of pieces. Then in a follow-up session, he played games in which he held up an instrument or played a rhythm and called on a child to give its name.

> As a part of his visits to a school, a composer asked children to sit very still in their room with their eyes closed, pick out a sound, then listen to all its changes during a two-minute period. He then gave the children an assortment of rubber bands, cups, lids, and boxes and asked them to invent a simple sound-maker. He asked them to experiment with all the different sounds they could produce. He played them a piece he had composed and talked with them about the patterns they could hear. Then he turned them back to their simple sound-makers and asked them to compose a piece in which they played with sounds and patterns.

In both the residencies, children were occupied and entertained. After all, each session was a switch from the ordinary. But the second experience is most likely to spark children's understanding of an art form. In the two examples, there is a real difference in the way that children are busy. In the first case, it is only the artist who has an active, aesthetic role. Children answer his questions and follow his example. In the second case, each child is involved in listening and composing. The artist takes the roles of a problem-poser, while children get the opportunity to solve those problems, each in his or her own way.

There is also a significant difference in what new information children are being exposed to. At first glance, the residency on Latin-American music seems to have much more to do with arts. After all, the children were actively taught the basic vocabulary of one kind of folk-music. By contrast, you might say that fooling around with rubber bands strung over cups was "beside the point" — what adult musician or composer fools around with that kind of twanging? But when you look deeper, the first artist is not introducing children to particularly artistic ways of listening or performing. Words like "marraca" and "samba" are being taught in much the same way that new words are learned for a spelling or vocabulary lesson.

It is true that the composer is not giving children hands-on experience with violins or musical scores, but this is because they simply do not have the skills or training to play musical instruments. What he is doing is using home-made instruments, simple as they are, as a means to offer children the chance to try out the kind of listening and composing that are at the heart of musical thinking.

So, when you plan an art experience for children, remember:

1. Children's, not just artists', aesthetic perceptions and abilities should get exercise.

2. The emphasis of the experience should fall on learning to work and think artistically. Guessing games, musical bingo, or vocabulary lessons may capture children's attention, but the bulk of skills, ideas, and perceptions taught should be artistic ones.

"Now That I Have Hired a Documentary Filmmaker, What Do I Do with Her?"

One thing everyone learns when putting together an arts program is that there are a dozen and one different kinds of artists. As one principal said, "I used to think that there were painters, actors, musicians, and dancers. Two months of planning and I know that there are photographers, media-artists, metal-workers, craftspeople. I'm beginning to suspect there are probably hummingbird feather-weavers that I ought to be considering."

No matter which kind of artist ends up on the roster, there is a fundamental issue to be considered: What are the likeliest and liveliest connections between that artist's skills and the curiosities, knowledge, and skills of the children with whom the artist will be working? To answer this question, you must consider three kinds of information: what artists can and want to do, what teachers hope for, and what children are like.

If you have hired a poet, then you have a "words-smith" coming to your school. Speak with teachers to find out what kinds of reading and writing children are able to handle, what kinds of literature and writing experiences they have planned, and what topics are being studied (e.g., the sea, dinosaurs, Eskimos, Native Americans). Offer the poet this information and talk together about the likely connections to his or her interests, skills and past experience in teaching children about creative writing. Before the poet arrives in class, he or she should spend time thinking about how his or her current interest in word play, the sea, or haiku poems can be translated into a writing experience that will engage and teach.

Once you know the general areas of the art form that the artist or performer would like to focus on, you can ask about other details that will have a bearing on how those skills will mesh with the regular school program. For example, in the case of the poet, you should find out what format he or she will want to use to work with children — Will it be one-on-one, small groups, or entire classrooms? Will it be for fifteen minutes a day or for long stretches of time to enable whole poems to get written? Experienced artists can outline their plans based on past experience. Less experienced artists can (and should) talk with teachers, parents, and artists who have seen what does and does not work well with children of various ages and abilities.

Now consider the likely connections between the artist's skills and interests and what teachers hope will happen. In the case of the poet, there are likely connections to language-learning activities such as talking, reading, writing, and listening. But you have hired an artist, not a speech therapist, so you should search out the teachers, classes, or children who are ripe for this especially rich opportunity to play and create with words. Ask around — there may be classroom teachers who have children keeping journals, who are writers themselves, who have asked for a writing residency in the past. Possibly, there are grades full of bi-lingual children where the issue of language is both lively and sensitive. Perhaps there is a graduating class that wants to write its own graduation play, rather than dragging out a tried and true classic.

When you are forging *connections*, do not be overly conventional in what you think of as "good links." It is not just the art teacher who might be eager to work with a sculptor. An industrial arts teacher might be very eager to work with a sculptor, especially one who uses plastics, welding, or casting. Students working on oral histories can make their work come alive if they are put in touch with a photographer who is interested in teaching them about photo essays. A weaver's patterns might spark curiosity and real problem solving in a geometry class. The key, however, is not to force connections where the participants see none. A math teacher might want to use weaving to teach about geometric patterns, but a particular weaver might feel that is uninteresting compared with teaching children about textures and colors.

Once you know what artists are eager to do and what interests teachers, find a way of putting them together. In some schools, teachers, parent coordinators, and artists meet to talk and generate ideas. In other schools, a coordinator talks with the artist, writes up a short description of proposed activities, sees that teachers each get a copy, and then collects specific requests and suggestions that are passed back to the artists.

When you are planning any performance, exhibit, or residency:

1. Find out what *specific* topics, skills, or processes the artist would like to share.

2. Search out the likely sites within the school where those (or similar) skills, topics, or processes would be met with enthusiasm.

3. Forge likely and lively connections between the artist's abilities and the school's interests.

WHAT KIND OF ART WHEN?

No amount of adult planning will ensure a successful artist visit if the ages, abilities, and interests of children are ignored. A graphic artist who specializes in teaching lithography is not well-suited to working with kindergartners, no matter how superb an artist or teacher he or she is. The lithography process is simply too complicated for five-year-olds to handle. An actor working in a middle school should know how to humor ten-year-old boys out of miserable self-consciousness and the belief that "you shouldn't talk to girls." If a painter begins with drawing exercises that are too "babyish," her class of high-school students may be hard to win back. The artists who have signed up to perform or teach are not mind readers or child psychologists. They often need help matching their artistic talents with the interests and maturity levels of children. Here are some suggestions:

Artists can pay a visit to the school *before* the residency takes place. The point of this first visit is, purely and simply, to see how particular children naturally use the skills that the artist will be working with later. This visit ought to be at a time when artists can have a close look at the children they might be working with — much like a tourist or an anthropologist in a new country. At some other time, the artist can meet the principal, find out where the bathrooms are, and get a parking sticker.

For example, a dancer might arrange to watch the way kids move up and down the halls, might sit in on basketball practice, or might look at the skateboard and bicycle hi-jinks that go on at recess. A writer could learn a lot from listening to show-and-tell or from observing the teasing and taunting of children as they wait for the buses. Sometimes an artist's reaction to this suggestions is, "Hey, look, I'm doing a residency, not a paper for Child Study 101." True enough — but artists who invest a morning or afternoon ahead of time find that they are tuned in to children's abilities, curiosities, customs, and cares in a way that makes a residency more than an exercise in survival. One writer who spent several hours in this way said, "It took the panic right out of 8:15 on the first morning. I had eaten lunch there on a Friday in February when all the menu said was 'cooks' surprise.' I had laughed all winter remembering the names kids had invented for that mysterious, grayish casserole. I was able to come in and tell them that poems weren't just about pretty flowers and kittens and sunsets. To prove it, I told them we were going to start by writing poems about school lunches."

Artists can learn a great deal from teachers. If they talk with either classroom, art, or music teachers, artists can find out what a group of children have been exposed to and about their interests and skills in a particular area. One side benefit of this kind of conference is that the potential tensions between teachers and visiting artists are channeled into a productive planning venture. A sculptor who was headed for his first residency in a middle school went to talk with the art teacher there. "She listened to my plans for 'getting kids to work in the round'. Then she offered to show me some slides of constructions kids in her classes had made. As they flashed on one after another, I began to see that kids that age weren't thinking abstractly about forms. They were working in the round, all right, but that was because their robot had a backpack or their dragon had four feet. If I hadn't seen those slides, I would have yakked them cross-eyed about the third dimension and got nowhere. Instead, we started with life-size science-fiction landscapes that you could walk through."

Artists can draw on another resource — their own recollections of what it was like to be a child. Especially important are recollections of what interested them about art when they were six or nine or fifteen. Possibly they have old photographs or drawings that can help them recapture what was puzzling or wonderful about sound, movement, paint, or clay when they were younger. Alternatively, artists may have friends who have worked with children of different ages in art schools, residencies, or summer camps who can share insights. Finding other colleagues to discuss these issues may be as easy as calling a community or state arts council which usually has records of residencies and performances. Consequently, the arts council staff can usually provide an artist with names and telephone numbers of other artists who have worked in a particular medium with a specific age-group. These people are an invaluable source of pointers, tips, and words to the wise.

"I HAVE MY SCULPTOR AND A ROOMFUL OF ELEVEN-YEAR-OLDS — NOW WHAT?"

Although reading is no substitute for experience, the materials on the next few pages suggest something about what children of different ages are like as makers and perceivers of artworks.

Five- to Eight-Year-Olds

One day I saw a giant
Many colored seagull in the sky.
It was floating in the Air
Some of the feathers fell
And I caught them
The feathers turned to water in my hand
It was a magic seagull.

Five- to Eight-Year-Olds

In these years, children make art as easily as they play kickball or pirates. They often take deep, uncritical pleasure in squeezing clay, dancing until they drop, putting on plays, or making huge free-form designs with poster paints. For most artists and performers, the issue is how to keep the lid on rather than how to get things started. But unlike preschoolers, five- to eight-year-olds care about their final products: they want to have clear, bright colors, costumes and audiences, glazes for their pottery. However, technical processes or abstract artistic problems confuse and bore them, so do not plan for sonnets and ballets. Instead, kindergarten, first, and second graders enjoy mastering direct, simple, concrete projects like hand-building with clay, block printing, knowing the steps of a folk dance, or composing rhythms.

From the time they were two and three, children have been communicating in all kinds of ways. Between five and eight they learn that some forms of communication, especially language and numbers, are more useful in school than others like drawing or dancing. The arts are especially powerful at this age because the presence of painters, craftspeople, actors, and dancers confirms the existence of many, varied modes of symbol use and self-expression. As children are asked to learn the difference between science and fantasy or counting and chanting, the arts can remind them how important imagination is.

Nine- to Eleven-Year-Olds

This is the age when children make collections, memorize all the elephant jokes, master the batting averages of all the players on their favorite baseball team, and have the lyrics to songs "by heart." Facts seem to replace intuitions and fantasies; children's self-consciousness about revealing their inner worlds grows. As young artists, children this age have to juggle the pleasures of invention with their impression that you have to draw horses just so, poems are supposed to rhyme, and films should be like what you see on TV.

During middle-school, children begin to make throughtful choices and judgments about artworks. While they may not use sophisticated terms, they begin to think, talk, or even argue about why a story is "really exciting" or "phony." At the same time, they can turn their standards on themselves and their peers so that artists have to be ready to break through statements like: "I'm no good," "It's too hard," or "She's better."

Nine-year-olds can turn to the arts to experience two quite different pleasures — the old zaniness and freedom to be like a "little kid" and a new zeal about skill, technique, and craft. The arts can make a tremendous difference to children in middle school by keeping them from becoming too factual, technical, and conventional. Expression, humor, and inventiveness are critical at a time when there is so much pressure, from within and without, to learn manners, rules, and conventions, and to be in control. Students may resist and hang back, not because they do not want to participate, but because of uncertainty and self-consciousness. It is important to be patient, not annoyed or angry. As an interesting and skilled adult, an artist can teach children about balancing craft with experiment, planning and playfulness, rules and inventions.

Nine- to Eleven-Year-Olds

Oh flashy clashy bike on the road.
your handle bars like wings,
you run like fire
and your tire is like wire.
you fly like fire under the telephone wire
oh flashing bike on the road

Twelve- to Fifteen-Year-Olds

Anger is like a hammer
pounding away at your heart
until you feel small.
It bends you out of shape.

As anger fades
the back of the hammer
pulls like pliers
at a rusty nail.
It's sharp at first,
but everyone is closer now.

Twelve- to Fifteen-Year-Olds

During these years, children are "betwixt and between"—not quite adults and certainly not "kids" any more. They are hungry for all kinds of grown-up skills, anything from dressing like adults to trying on ideas. While the adult world is exciting, it is also demanding. Between twelve and fifteen, most young adolescents see-saw back and forth between impulse and spontaneity on the one hand and thinking, watching, and wondering on the other.

Figuring out the world "out there" is not all that is on young teenagers' minds. There is also the giant task of figuring themselves out — what do they like, want, trust, see themselves becoming? In these years the arts provide students with powerful ways of reflecting on themselves and capturing what is beginning to be a personal point of view. The arts can offer adolescents a place to try out personal visions rather than conventional or "gang" definitions of what's right or cool. However, teenagers may need privacy, practice and peer support before they will take the "risk" of going public with a painting, story, or sculpture. They may feel safer behind a camera, throwing a pot, or performing someone else's dance. Because self-consciousness is extreme at this age, it is often useful to have a range of projects, arts forms, and techniques so that students do not feel trapped in an activity they think will make them appear stupid or incompetent. Keep in mind, too, that in early adolescence, children are old enough to take genuine pleasure out of artistic perception as well as artistic production. They are more sensitive to artistic messages and styles and should be given an opportunity to listen, to watch, and to discuss what they have experienced and what it means to them.

Sixteen- to Eighteen-Year-Olds

At the end of high-school, adolescents have to face real rather than day-dreamy questions about what they will do and who they will be. At one and the same time, they are both fiercely critical and idealistic. They are self-aware enough to know what they would like to do and be. But more than ever, they realize the obstacles that sit between what they hope for and what they will probably get: race, gender, social class, and training. Artists working in high schools often confront a sharp division between students who have interest and students who do not see why they should care about trying to dance or write music.

Whether or not individuals are going to become artists — and most will not — they can learn to take pleasure in things they make, choose, or behold. Time with adults who value aesthetic experience "says" that this kind of caring about artistic experience is valuable, important, and enjoyable. Moreover, discipline and work in the service of trying to create or communicate is a concept older adolescents can grasp.

Sixteen- to Eighteen-Year-Olds

Time

We laughed and spoke and smiled and made
A gold and green world of light and shade.
A secret world - if only you had stayed.

Time will find the ache and still it,
Search out the void and gently fill it,
Time will fill my days - or will it?

BETWEEN CONTRACT AND CLEAN-UP:
AMPLIFYING THE EFFECTS OF AN ARTIST'S VISIT

No yeast — no bread; no fertilizer — no bumper crop; no preparation or follow-up — no lasting effects of artists' visits to schools. You might think you are finished with planning once artists and teachers outline the contents of upcoming visits. But if you include two additional steps in your planning process, you can amplify the excitement and learning generated.

We are all familiar with the idea of warming up: dancers stretch and bend before trying jumps, kindergarten is a warm-up for the routines and skills of first grade. By the same token, before going to an opera, you may warm up by reading the story so that you can listen to the music during the performance. Similarly, children who are about to spend time with an artist will be better able to make the leap to new routines, skills, and information if they have had the chance to warm up. Preparations for an artist's visit can include any number of things: helping children to think about what art is, about a particular art-form, about the individual artist who is coming, about the actual project that artists and teachers have planned. No matter how restricted time and money are, it is possible to do some spade work.

Just to prove the point, consider the preparation work for a film-maker's residency done by two middle-school teachers in a tiny rural school with an art teacher who visited once a month, a town library open from 1 - 4 on Wednesdays, and an old, but workable, film projector.

> Once we knew we had landed the residency, we began to plan. We set aside an hour a week for projects we called "Film-Works." We really only had the film catalogue from the state university and everyone's television to work with. To start with, we had the students read a short story and then watch a film made from that story. That week we talked about the special qualities of films as compared to pictures or books. Another week we asked students to watch a science documentary about the ocean on TV and in class we saw an art film about the sea. We talked that afternoon about special effects and how they created moods. Another time we gave them cardboard squares with small holes to act like lenses, so they could experiment with "close-ups," angles, and distance viewing in order to get a feel for the choices an artist makes using a camera. When the residency actually began, the students were really excited; they couldn't wait to get started.

Just as important as preparation of this sort is the follow-up of an arts-in-education experience. It is easy to assume that when the curtain comes down or the drawings are taken down off the walls, that "that's all, folks" — at least until the next artist is hired. But the process of following up on an artist's visit can reinforce or amplify the effect of that visit. Follow-up can be as simple as bringing up an idea, a character, or a speech from a play the following day. This kind of mention suggests to children that adults attend carefully to, enjoy, and remember art works. Talking with children about their responses to films, dances, or sculptures carries much the same message. In planning this simple kind of follow-up, remember that the point is to heighten or extend children's enjoyment or understanding of the arts. Enforced "thank-you" notes copied from a text printed on the blackboard are unlikely to draw out the excitement, interest, or inventiveness children may have experienced.

More promising possibilities include: encouraging children to write or dictate personal accounts of what they saw, heard, or felt during the artist's visit; including some of the same materials or techniques that a visual artist had introduced in classes; and taking the opportunity to look at more works in the same art form, including viewing dances on film, paintings in books, music on recordings. People other than teachers can contribute to follow-up activities. The school librarian can display books on crafts following a potter's residency. A parent can read aloud one afternoon a week to keep alive what children learned working with a writer. Older students can work with younger ones to write down chants and songs they learned to value through a composer's visit.

Artists' visits can be amplified outside of classrooms, too. Sometimes these activities are quite closely tied to the specific residency. For example, following his residency at an elementary school, a painter invited his class to come on a field trip to his house. He showed them not just where he painted and cooked and watched television, but places near his house where he went to sketch. As they left, he provided students with materials to sketch. The following week, the art teacher worked with children helping them to use their sketches and memories of the outdoors to make paintings. These were exhibited, along with the artist's sketches in the front hall of the school. At another school, parents drove students to a gallery where they saw "their" glassblower's work on display.

Artist's visits can also provide a starting point for exploring a range of artistic resources within a community. After working with a jazz quartet, a group of high school students became fascinated with investigating all the different musical styles that could be found in their small city. As a project for their social studies class, they located and recorded different musicians from French-Canadian folk singers to black gospel singers and interviewed them about where and how they learned their music.

As a part of planning artist visits to schools:

1. Prepare children — invent ways for them to become informed and excited about their chance to work with artists.

2. Follow up on work artists have done — discover ways to amplify and extend what children have taken away from the visit or performance.

BUT WHO CAN REMEMBER TO DO ALL THAT?

Quite possibly, this all sounds like too much to remember, much less to accomplish. In a way, artist visits and residencies are artistic productions. If they are to be lively and valuable, they demand planning, creativity, revision, and polishing (in other words, a lot of work). If you boil the process of planning artist's visits down to essentials, these are the steps:

1. Decide whether you want to plan for exposure or immersion programs.

2. Work with artists and teachers to ensure the *artistic* purposes of the visit.

3. Forge likely and lively connections between the skills and interests of the artist and those of teachers and parents.

4. Design programs suited to the interests and abilities of the children involved.

5. Prepare children (and the larger school community).

6. Plan to amplify the effects of the visit.

Chapter 5
Fund Raising

by Thomas Wolf

Martha Brown is a very frustrated person. She has been the head of the Parent-Teacher Organization at her children's school for two years. Before that she was the Chairperson of the Arts Committee. She *knows* what a terrific program the organization has offered over the last several years. Yet, when she sends out a letter asking individuals, businesses, and foundations to support the program, she receives almost no response. Worse yet, fund raising is the one area where no one volunteers to help her out. When she requests volunteers to host visiting artists and musicians, everyone seems interested. Blank stares follow her requests for fund-raising volunteers. Her problem is compounded by the fact that the state arts council, which has been supporting her program for years, has told her that the state support will be gradually phased out and that she must begin to find private support in the community.

Martha Brown's experience is not unusual. Nor are her difficulties hard to understand. Like most people responsible for running arts-in-education programs, she knows a lot about the arts but not very much about fund raising. Because she is an expert about her program and is committtted to it, she assumes others will also be interested and want to support it. But she forgets that other people may have their own causes and that it will take a lot of persuasion to get them to support another organization to which they have no particular connection. She keeps hoping that someone with lots of money will come around and see what a great job is being done and want to help out with funding. But deep down she knows that this probably will not happen and wonders what she should be doing to make the fund-raising effort a success.

If all of this seems unpleasantly familiar, the following chapter is for you. It may not turn you into a fund raiser, but it should help you to learn what an organization needs to do to be successful in attracting funds.

WHAT BASICS SHOULD YOU KNOW ABOUT FUND RAISING BEFORE YOU BEGIN?

First, be sure you recognize three basic truths about fund raising:

— There are always more good causes than can possibly be supported.

— No one will ever be as enthusiastic about your project as you are.

— People like to feel involved in those causes that they support.

The easiest way to remember these truths is to imagine yourself in the position of people being asked for money. Regardless of who they are, it is likely that they are receiving many more requests than they can possibly say "yes" to. A wealthy individual just before the end of the calendar year might easily receive ten fund-raising letters *every day*. A corporate contributions officer might be required to review over 500 requests each month spanning the fields of education, health, social services, and the arts and humanities. Is it any surprise that your request does not seem to amaze and impress them? Others with equally good projects are knocking on the same door. To you, your project is unique; to someone who is deciding whether to give you money, yours is just one of many possible projects competing for limited funds.

On the other hand, while your project may not overpower prospective donors, they may be impressed with you personally — with your commitment, enthusiasm, organizational abilities and, perhaps most important, your interest in *their* ideas. Keep in mind that the people from whom you are requesting money must make a difficult decision about which organizations to support. And it is quite likely that the programs that will be supported are those in which the donors feel some personal connection to the activity, the organization, or the person or persons asking for the money. It is only human nature for donors to be responsive to those who show an interest in their ideas and opinions as well as in their money. A form letter, sent out without even a personal note attached, will not make people feel part of the project and organization. Consider this case:

> A school planning to build a new arts facility sent out a prospectus and fund-raising letter to parents. One wealthy parent with a well-known professional interest in the arts did not respond. The Chairperson of the Fund-Raising Committee followed up with a personal visit, during which the prospective donor said that he had no intention of contributing. The school had had an opportunity to ask his advice before going ahead with the plans for the building. He had read the prospectus, was unhappy with certain decisions, and so was not going to contribute to something he did not believe in. Instead, he had decided to support several other organizations that had solicited him for funds. The Fund-Raising Committee Chair-

person reported back to the Building Committee Chairperson who was sufficiently concerned to pay a second visit to the prospective donor. After a three-hour session in which the two discussed the plans in some detail, the donor pledged $1,000 to the building fund. He confessed that he had been surprised that he had not been invited to make some suggestions in the planning phase but had been even more put out when he had subsequently been solicited for a sizable donation through a form letter. "If you want my money," he said, "then it is only fair to treat me like a *person*."

WHERE DO YOU BEGIN?

The easiest way to prepare yourself for fund raising is to complete a fund-raising "information inventory." Such an inventory is a lot less forbidding than it sounds. It is simply a series of basic planning questions to ask yourself and people in your organization. The questions are:

1. How much money do we need to run the program? (Good budgeting is absolutely necessary *before* fund raising begins.)

2. How much will the school (or school district) contribute? (Many donors will not be enthusiastic if the school is contributing nothing. Often, though, a non-cash donation of release time, space, or equipment is sufficient indication of the school's commitment.)

3. What specific activities do we need the money for? (Having a list of activities can be useful when you are asking people for money; the more specific your request, often the more successful you will be.)

4. What kinds of "fund raisers" (bake sales, auctions, calendars, car washes) are planned and how much will they bring in? (Because "fund raisers" can drain energy and time from your volunteer pool, be sure that they really do have a financial payoff.)

5. How much help can you count on in fund raising? (If the answer is "not very much," you may want to organize a fund-raising committee and solicit additional help *before* you begin — fund raising needs many people.)

6. Who has supported you in the past and are they likely to support you again? (Your best prospects are those who have a history of support; concentrate on getting this group to increase their contributions.)

7. Who might be likely to support you for the first time? (Make a list of those who are already familiar with your program, are friendly with people in your organization, or are generally interested in arts-in-education.)

8. What is your "case for support"? (Make a list of aspects of your program that are unique and special. Be as specific as possible.)

9. What would you spend money on if you had more money than you needed? (It is useful to have a "wish list" and a longer-range plan so you can talk about things other than immediate needs with potential donors.)

After you have completed the information inventory and analyzed it carefully, you are ready to plan your fund-raising activities in more detail.

Other Kinds of Assistance

There is another important thing to remember as you begin your efforts to put the organization and its program on a firm financial footing: Knowing ways to *save* money is as important as knowing how to raise money. Of two organizations sponsoring a photography residency, one raised a good deal of money so that equipment could be rented and film could be purchased. The other organization borrowed cameras from the state arts council, secured free film from the Polaroid Foundation and a local merchant, borrowed enlargers from the local YMCA, and got the school to build a makeshift, portable darkroom from aluminum pipes and heavy dark fabric. The resourcefulness of the second organization took some of the strain off the fund-raising committee.

There are other examples of ways of saving money: getting reduced prices from merchants, securing donations of scraps and discards from manufacturers, bartering and exchanging items with schools and other nonprofit organizations, and obtaining free publicity in a merchant's regular advertising space in the local newspaper. In addition, the organization should attempt to get as much free help as possible in bookkeeping and accounting, legal assistance, promotion, and other areas in which a board member might contribute such expertise.

HOW CAN YOU GET MONEY FOR ARTS-IN-EDUCATION PROGRAMS?

There are two basic ways to get money for your program:

—you can *earn* it

or

—you can *raise* it

Earning money might include charging an admission fee for events, selling memberships in your organization, offering donated merchandise or services

for sale or resale. Raising money includes soliciting contributions or grants from your school district, from individuals, businesses, foundations, and from government agencies at the federal, state, or local level.

Earning Money

Many organizations that present arts-in-education programs are proud that everything they offer is free. Charging for an activity would be an anathema to them because they feel that charging would undermine the quality of what is presented and would prevent certain people from being able to attend or participate in events and opportunities. Such an attitude, however, bears careful scrutiny. There are many activities that an organization can sponsor that are income producing at the same time that they provide something of quality and importance to the community.

Consider this case: An organization in a small community was accustomed to bringing in musicians for five-day residencies in the schools. For several years, the final residency event was a free concert for the community. When finances got tight, the organization was faced with a choice: either abandon the community concert entirely or charge admission. It was decided that tickets would be sold for the concert but that senior citizens and students would continue to receive free admission. The decision turned out to be a good one for three reasons: audience numbers *increased*, a new source of cash was added to the organization's coffers, and funding sources were persuaded that the community really wanted the concert since members of the audience were willing to pay for it.

In thinking about whether to charge for things, the following point should be kept in mind: In the funding community today, there is often a bias against organizations that have no source of earned income. This bias stems from a concern that when things are free, it is often difficult to assess whether people really want them. Obviously, you do not want to exclude people from programs simply because they cannot afford them; but there may be ways to charge certain people for some things. Your organization should examine this possibility carefully before deciding that everything should be free.

There are other ways to earn money that do not involve charging for events. Sometimes these entrepreneurial efforts involve ingenuity and hard work on the part of kids involved in the arts program. In one Rhode Island high school, for example, members of the student council earned over $5,000 for an artist residency program through the sale of health food snacks. Students oversaw the acquisition of food, did all the selling, and kept the books. Another school runs a paperback bookstore and turns the profit over to the arts program. Because the store is staffed by parent-volunteers, the overhead is low and the income derived is considerable. A third school has combined an arts activity with a source of earned income. Each Christmas, the art teacher selects outstanding student work and prints up a giant school calendar that sells for $5.00. Over $2,500 each year is earned through this effort.

Raising Money

The other way to secure funds for your program is to fund-raise. There are numerous approaches:

1. **Fund-Raising Events** - There are countless examples of these events to raise cash and most can be fun. School fairs, auctions in which parents donate and then bid on goods and services (such as baked goods or babysitting), dinner dances, concert benefits, and the like can provide cash while also offering an opportunity for young and old in the community to come together and have a good time. One group of fourth graders needed $300 for a film-making project and came up with the idea of a community car wash. It took only two Saturdays to wash enough cars to raise the needed cash. One nice aspect of fund-raising events is that they provide some form of unrestricted earned income — that is, money that can be used for any aspect of the program. By way of contrast, much of the money that is contributed by donors is restricted for a specific activity or purpose.

2. **Fund-Raising Letters** - Almost anyone who fund-raises extensively does some of it through letters. However, most beginners rely far too heavily on this approach. The most effective letters are ones in which a personal message is sent from someone that the prospective contributor knows. Form letters, when they must be used, are usually most effective with people who already have a history of giving to the organization. An effort should be made to put a personal message (often a personal "P.S." is adequate) on as many letters as possible. One young volunteer sent a particularly personal and effective note to her fiance that resulted in a sizable donation. The message read: "Roses are red / Violets are blue / If you don't donate some money / I won't marry you."

3. **Face-to-Face Solicitation** - This approach is most effective because it allows a give-and-take between the fund raiser and the donor. Large gifts from individuals (over $100) should be solicited this way whenever possible. One good strategy is to invite the donor to an activity at the school and then discuss the possibility of a contribution when the excitement of the program is fresh in the donor's mind. Incidently, the old adage about "taking a donor to lunch" is not always advisable. Potential donors are often busy people. Be sure you use their time to good advantage.

4. **Telephone Solicitation** - Telephone solicitation is an intermediate approach that has the advantage of personal give-and-take between caller and donor yet is more efficient and less time-consuming than face-to-face

solicitation. It is often most effective when it is linked to a special fund-raising drive that the donor is told about before hand (often through a brief letter). It is also advantageous if the person calling is a volunteer who shares some important characteristic with the donor (they have children in the same class, they went to the same college, they are members of the same church). Telephone solicitation allows the caller to be enthusiastic about the program and allows the donor to speak his or her mind to a willing listener.

5. **Proposal Writing** - Many public agencies, corporations, and foundations require that you submit a written proposal if you want to receive money from them. But *beware*! Every proposal must be customized to the requirements and interests of the potential donor. Do not, under any circumstances, type up a proposal that you copy and send to a number of potential funders. You will not even raise enough money in this way to pay for your postage. Rather, make sure you have discussed a proposal in depth with the potential funder before you write a single word.

HOW IMPORTANT IS IT TO GET A CONTRIBUTION FROM THE SCHOOL OR SCHOOL DISTRICT?

Most funders want to see a commitment of some sort from school officials for your program. It is best, of course, to be able to show that the school or district has budgeted actual cash toward the program, but, when this is not possible, it is absolutely essential to show that there is at least some form of a non-cash (or what is called "in-kind") contribution. Some examples of this include donated artist supplies, teacher release time, contributed studio space, or use of school buses for trips. Without even these kinds of donations from the school, a funder might have a legitimate question about the school's interest in the program and the program's long-term chances of success. Thus, it is worth making a substantial effort to get the school to come up with a contribution.

In most cases, this is far easier said than done. The case for funding arts programs is often a difficult one to argue before school boards and school administrators. Some arguments for support have been presented in Chapter 1. However, beyond the arguments themselves, there are certain important strategies for getting funding from schools and school districts:

1. **Plan Ahead** - School budgeting is done far ahead of time, and once budget decisions are made they are difficult if not impossible to change. Your planning and advocacy work should begin a full year ahead of the budget year you are attempting to influence.

2. **Find a Budget Insider** - Attempt to find a sympathetic friend of your program who understands the budgeting process and the budget itself. Find out what is the best strategy for influencing the budgeting process. Who are the key decision makers and what are their interests? Figure out whether the arts program can be described to be consistent with those interests.

3. **Analyze the Budget** - Find how the budget is organized, and figure out whether there are already discretionary items in which your arts program can be placed. (Remember, it is always easier to build yourself into an existing category of the budget than to create a new one.) Have your "budget insider" suggest the best strategy.

4. **Build an Advocacy Network** - If it is true that the squeaky wheel gets the grease, it is also true that the loudest and largest constituency gets the largest share of a school or school district's discretionary dollars. Your case can be convincing, but if you do not have a large group of parents pressing for the school program, your request for funds or in-kind donations will probably fall on deaf ears.

5. **Meet with the Decision Makers before the Decision** - Attempt to influence the outcome of the decision-making process by talking to those who will be making the decision. It is important to understand where they are coming from. If the image of the school is important to one person, talk about the arts almost always being associated with top school systems and having good public relations value. If another decision maker is interested in basic skills, talk about the link between the arts and cognitive development. Try to have all of your allies in place before a decision is put to a vote.

In the end, it is important to make arts funding a regular part of the school or school district's budget. You should always have someone in your organization monitoring the budgeting process and building a support network for either establishing, maintaining, or increasing the line item for arts programs in the budget. Do not make the mistake of assuming that once you have dollars in the budget, your problems are over. Discretionary funds come out of budgets more easily than they go in. Each year you will have to fight to make sure your school support will be there.

HOW DO YOU IDENTIFY INDIVIDUALS TO ASK FOR MONEY?

There is a fundamental rule of fund raising: *only prospectors find gold*. Good fund raisers, like prospectors, spend much of their time

searching out potential contributors. They know that more than half of the battle is identifying those from whom they will seek funds. A good fund raiser is easy to spot. He or she is the one who saves symphony orchestra or theatre programs in order to check the contributor list; reads the newspaper to find out which of the local businesses have supported educational programs or other activities for kids; and picks other people's brains to discover who they know who might be a potential contributor.

How can you become a "prospector"? Your own mailing list, if you have one, is a good place to start. It should tell you who has asked to receive information about your program, attended events, or participated in your activities. All of these people are potential contributors. If you do not have a mailing list, start one. Every time someone makes an inquiry or expresses an interest in what you are doing, ask for a name, address, and phone number. A small percentage of these people may actually turn into contributors. Others may help you *identify* people who might contribute. Do not be shy about asking for money and help. Remember that your easiest selling job is to those already interested in your program. The worst thing that can happen when you ask for help or money is that the person will say "no," and, except for some ego bruising, a "no" doesn't really hurt.

Another way to find potential donors is to beg, borrow, or buy the mailing or donor list of another organization whose philanthropic purposes are similar to yours. Getting your hands on an actual mailing list may be difficult (organizations tend to be fairly secretive with this information), but getting a list of names may be as simple as picking up the organization's annual report or promotional literature and locating the list of contributors. Addresses will not be available when you get the list in this fashion, but you can always look up the addresses in the telephone directory. Remember that almost no one contributes to only one organization. People who donate money generally spread it around. Thus, your strategy should be to find those who are already philanthropically inclined and then from that group to identify those who are interested in the arts or in education.

As your fund-raising efforts get going, keep detailed records on those who contribute and those who do not. This will allow you gradually to convert your mailing list into a detailed, annotated donor list. For each contributor, you should keep information on the years in which they were solicited, how much they gave, and what the money was used for. This will help you as you plan your fund-raising efforts for future years. Knowing that someone has consistently contributed to crafts residencies, for example, would suggest that this person might not be the best prospect for underwriting a concert series. By the same token, knowing that someone has contributed $250 in a previous year indicates that solicitation for the current year's gift should be planned carefully, probably done in person, and geared around a minimum gift of $250.

Individuals usually provide the largest source of contributed dollars—particularly "no strings attached" (or unrestricted) dollars. Spending time and effort in building a good donor list is important. Though it may take months and even years to get the list to a point where it starts producing for you, the effort is well worth your time.

SHOULD YOU EXPECT TO GET MONEY FROM THE BUSINESS COMMUNITY?

The business community has at its disposal a great deal of money. But getting your hands on that money is not easy. The purpose of a business is to turn a profit, not to give its money away. Large corporations are expected to make money and return some of it to their shareholders. Their purposes are not essentially philanthropic. Nevertheless, businesses do support nonprofit organizations in the arts-in-education field. They do so for a variety of reasons and may donate money if:

—the program is good for the community.

—the program offers a particular benefit to the corporation's employees.

—the program offers the corporation high visibility and serves its public relations.

Local Business

Your most likely success will be with your local business community. Here you should strive for a large number of small annual gifts. This is because it is difficult to secure large corporate gifts year after year and the large gifts that you do secure are often for special projects that do not help you pay your basic operating costs. You can more realistically expect to raise small sums year after year from a variety of businesses and, if you have organized your campaign correctly, you can use the money where you need it. Think of it this way: It would be very difficult, if not impossible, to find a business that would contribute $5,000 to your organization. However, it is not improbable that you could convince twenty businesses to contribute $50 each year for five years and bring in the same $5,000. And the money would probably be unrestricted. There are a couple of important tips to bear in mind as you raise money from the local business community:

1. If at all possible, your business fund raising should be done by members of the business community — peer to peer. This means that

you must secure some business allies who are willing to write letters, make telephone calls, and visit with their colleagues on your behalf.

2. If you are raising money for a particular event or series of events, prepare a fact sheet that includes:
— name of school(s)
— name of artist(s) with brief statement of credentials
— date(s)
— brief description of what is to take place
— list of what groups will benefit
— publicity plans (including how the business will be thanked)
— budget
— list of other contributors
(Do remember, though, that you want to keep the business contributions as unrestricted as possible, so only specify which event a particular business is being asked to fund if it is clear that this is the only way you will get the funding.)

3. Any additional written material in business fund raising should be *brief*. A one-page, attractively printed description of your program plus a cover letter is sufficient, particularly since most first-time contributors should have been contacted initially by phone or in person.

4. Secure a fifteen- or twenty-minute presentation slot at some regularly scheduled business lunches. If possible, put on a light and entertaining program showing what your organization does. (One arts-in-education organization presents a program annually for the Rotary Club in its community in which musicians perform and share some of the more humorous experiences from their work with school children.) At the end of the program, tell the audience that a member of the business community will be contacting them to ask for their support.

5. Be sure that you have some way of acknowledging business contributions publicly. If you present events that have printed programs, be sure to list your supporters prominently. Mention them in newspaper stories. Invite representatives of the business community to selected activities and, if they come, thank them publicly.

6. If appropriate, ask for things other than cash. It is a lot less expensive for a restaurant to give you $50 worth of meals for your artist than to contribute $50 in cash. A building supply company can contribute $50 worth of lumber less expensively than the equivalent amount in cash. If you need the merchandise or the services that a business has to offer, ask for them.

7. Once a business is a regular annual contributor, you should design your request for the next annual contribution in such a way that

it is easier for the business to say "yes" than to say "no." One summer arts organization sends out a letter in March to all of its previous year's business contributors. The letter states that if they do not hear from the business by April 1, they will assume that a gift can be expected and will instruct the printer to list the business on the organization's promotional flyer. The business is then invoiced in July and the printed flyer is included in the envelope. Many business people appreciate the convenience of the system, although it is true that a few end up not contributing. Nevertheless, the system saves everyone a great deal of time and effort.

8. Thank contributors promptly for their gifts. Thank them again a few months later by updating them on the progress of the program or sending along a newspaper article or promotional brochures. It is important to make your contributors feel a part of your activities and to be in touch with them at times other than when you are asking for money.

Corporate Gifts

Large corporations with active giving programs generally wish to achieve great impact and high visibility through their contributions. Most often they make large gifts to large organizations. Because of the sheer numbers involved, it is not cost efficient for them to consider applications from tiny organizations. There are exceptions, of course, but the percentages are not in favor of your organization receiving a contribution from a major corporation. The one exception to this rule is if the corporate headquarters happens to be located in your home town or if a significant number of employees live there. This improves your chances, but it is probably not advantageous to spend a lot of time working on corporate proposals.

If you do decide to undertake a corporate proposal, attempt to see the corporate contributions officer first. It is helpful if you can secure a referral from someone who knows or has worked with that person. Then simply call up and say that Mr. X recommended that you call and request a couple of minutes of the officer's time to find out more about the corporation's contributions policy. If you do get an appointment, be brief. Attempt to get the contributions officer to do most of the talking. Find out where his or her interests lie, what kind of a proposal would meet with the greatest chance of success, how much you should ask for, whether there is a particularly good time to submit the proposal, what format is most desirable (a letter, an application form, a proposal narrative), and what supplementary material will be required.

Do keep in the back of your mind, though, that a corporate gift is probably a long shot and your budget should not be constructed around the idea that such a gift will be forthcoming.

thank you

How Should You Write a Proposal and When Should You Use It?

There are times when you will be expected to write a formal funding proposal. Sometimes the funding source will provide an application form with spaces and blanks requesting specific narrative and budget information. This is particularly common with public agencies like state arts councils, the National Endowment for the Arts, and other governmental units. Often, though, you will be given little or no guidance. You will be told by a foundation, by a corporation, even, occasionally, by an individual, to "submit a written proposal."

The first rule of thumb is to find out as much as possible about what the funder is looking for in the proposal. How long should it be? How should it be organized? What should be stressed? Every proposal should be tailored to the idiosyncracies of a particular funding source. The second important rule is to keep the proposal as short as possible. A corporation rarely wants to see more than three or four pages of narrative plus budget. You can and should send supplementary material — such as a brochure, annual report, or letters of support — but the proposal itself should be short, clearly and simply written, and easy to scan. "If you can't scan it, can it," says one experienced fund raiser. He adds: "I always begin the proposal with an introduction which is no longer than one page, gives all the pertinent information, and is presented in giant-sized type. This page is often all that the person looking at the proposal will read carefully, so I am careful to make it clear and succinct."

A proposal generally consists of the following elements:
— an introduction or abstract
— a problem statement
— goals and objectives of the project
— a capability statement
— a detailed program description
— a budget

The *introduction* should be very short — sometimes a single paragraph will do. It should give the essentials: who is asking for the money and how much is being requested, what the money will be used for, what the starting and ending dates of the project will be, what will be accomplished, who will provide other funds. The material that you collected for your fact sheet in raising money from local businesses can provide some of the background material for the introduction as well. Do *not* give a history of the organization either here or elsewhere in the proposal. The proposal should describe what you are intending to do, not what you have done.

The *problem statement* briefly outlines the general problem this project will address. Some examples might be inadequate time and money for arts exposure in the schools, few opportunities for kids to hear live music or see an artist at work, no chance for teachers to work with artists in order to integrate arts experiences into their own classroom teaching, not enough employment for outstanding artists and performers in the region. Two problems can be related in your statement in such a way that the project you are proposing solves both at the same time. For example, one organization that wanted to secure funds for a music education program in one rural county in New England wrote: "In our county, three out of every four graduating seniors has never heard a live musical concert. At the same time, few first-year graduates of our leading conservatories find adequate employment opportunities on the concert stage." This sets the stage for the next section of the proposal, which sets out exactly how these problems can be solved.

The *goals and objectives* section should relate directly to the problem statement and tell what the general intent of the program will be (the goals) and what specific steps will be taken to accomplish them (the objectives). In the previous example, the goals of the project were to bring more live music to the county's schools *and* to provide more employment opportunities for the young conservatory graduates of the region. The objectives were to serve twenty-five communities with at least one arts exposure per child during a two-year period and to provide no less than $2,000 in concert income to fifteen musicians performing in the schools during the same period. Note in this case how general is the statement of goals and how specific, quantifiable and measurable are the objectives. In evaluating the project, you are going to have to show that the specific objectives that you set for yourself have been achieved. So be realistic! There is nothing wrong with exceeding projections; it is more embarrassing to fall short of what you said you would do.

A *capability statement* answers the question that the potential funder asks: "Why should your organization be chosen to do this project?" The funder may agree that the problems you have cited need addressing, but this does not necessarily mean that there is not another organization that could do as good if not better job. Here you must point to your track record, perhaps a few achievements, awards, and successes. Explain the ways in which your organization is unique (e.g., the only organization with the school superintendent on the Board of Directors, the only organization that has provided in-school enrichment programs for fifteen years in your community, the only arts organization to have received the Mayor's Distinguished Service Award). A second tack here is to talk about the cost effectiveness of working through your organization. Sure, others may be able to provide the same services. But they cannot provide the same level of service for the same price. You might also mention that your organization has the best chance of leveraging such matching funds from a variety of public and private sources if this is in fact the case.

Depending on the scope of your proposal, you may be asked to provide a detailed *program description*. Before you launch into a long description of how you will proceed and who will be involved, be certain just what the funder needs and wants. The program description is one area where proposal writers hurt their chances by making the proposal too long. Often all that is needed is a brief outline of what will happen month-by-month (or, on shorter, more concentrated projects, week-by-week). Sometimes brief biographical descriptions (or resumes) of key personnel are requested. If the program description becomes too long, include it as an appendix or attachment. At every opportunity, ask yourself, Is this really needed? Is the proposal getting too long?

Before you end your proposal, you should include a brief *evaluation plan*. This plan will state exactly how you plan to determine whether or not your program was a success. Funders like to see more than a descriptive kind of evaluation plan. It is no longer acceptable simply to include some cute letters from children saying how much they liked the program. You must set some quantifiable objectives, as was discussed in the *objectives* section, and see whether you achieve them.

Make sure that it will not be too difficult to collect the information you need for your evaluation. If one of your targets is twenty-five concerts, it is a simple matter to count whether or not you presented that number of concerts. But if your target is improving reading scores among kids exposed to the program, you will have to set up a complicated system involving an "exposure" group and a "control" group, you will have to test children before and after the program, and you will need to score the tests and do quite a bit of paper work. Evaluation plans should be as simple as possible so that you do not put more effort into evaluation than into the program itself.

The *budget* section is one of the most misunderstood areas of proposal writing. Many people believe that an organization needs to show a deficit in order to ask for money. But many nonprofit organizations run at a surplus for many years, putting their extra money away into an endowment or reserve fund. The reason they can do this and still show the potential funding source a deficit budget is that they offer a "project budget" that simply summarizes the income and expense for the activity for which they are raising the money. If an arts-in-education organization is trying to raise money for a residency, for example, and if it looks like a particular funding source might give $2,000 toward this residency, then the residency budget should be designed in order to show that projected income is $2,000 less than projected expenses. If other activities such as the bake sale, the annual appeal letter, and other fund-raising efforts end up producing more money than expected, it is perfectly legal to put this money into a reserve account at the bank. Avoid presenting the organization's total budget when it is more appropriate to present simply a budget for the project itself. The organization might be bringing in an overall surplus for the year, but the funding source should be shown the residency budget that requires $2,000.

Once your proposal is finished, three additional items should be included with it in a "proposal package:"

1. A cover letter written on the organization's letterhead that refers to the enclosed proposal and states where you can be reached if there are any questions. (It is desirable for your Board members to be listed on your letterhead. If they are not, include this list separately.)

2. A financial statement showing a review of the organization's fiscal activities for the most recently completed fiscal year. For large organizations ($50,000 or over) this should be an audited statement. Sometimes the funding source may also ask you to include your tax determination letter from the Internal Revenue Service proving that you are tax-exempt.

3. A public relations brochure describing your organization. If you do not have such a printed piece, you can include a couple of letters of support from key people in the school and community, press clippings, and the like. But do not bury the package with such material.

Your proposal is now complete. Check it to make sure the budget is figured correctly, that the language is clear and simple, and that there are no errors in the text. If the proposal seems overly long, cut it. Always err on the side of brevity and simplicity.

There is one more essential thing you must know about fund raising. Even skilled fund raisers hear the word "no" more often than the word "yes." Good fund raising is a numbers game. If you identify fifty prospects, end up talking to thirty, and ask twenty for money, you may be lucky enough to get ten contributions. That means that forty people in one way or another are going to say "no" to you. Do not get discouraged and above all *do not take a "no" personally*. A good fund raiser should have an automatic translator in the brain that converts the word "no" to "come back another time." Experience shows that the prospect who says "no" this year will, with proper care and feeding, become a contributor next year or sometime in the future. Indeed, if you can master your disappointment and vow to be persistent, you will have learned the most fundamental secret of good fund raising.

Arts in Education: A Selected Bibliography

Compiled by Sharon Hya Grollman

PART I: PUBLICATIONS

The Arts, Education, and Americans: A Series of Arts in Education Monographs,
1981-1982. AEA, John F. Kennedy Center for the Performing Arts, Washington, D.C. 20566

Number 1 - *People and Places: Reaching Beyond the Schools*
Describes how several school districts expanded their arts programs by reaching out and using community resources.

Number 2 - *Your School District and the Arts: A Self-Assessment*
Provides suggestions for arts advocates for checking on the quality of arts programs in rural, suburban, and city schools.

Number 3 - *Local School Boards and the Arts: A Call for Leadership*
Examines how school board members can promote arts programs.

Number 4 - *Ideas and Money for Expanding School Arts Programs*
A catalogue of resources for use in developing and supporting school arts programs.

Number 5 - *Method and the Muse: Planning a School Arts Program*
A step-by-step guide to planning a school arts program.

Number 6 - *Developing Financial Resources for School Arts Programs*
Offers a variety of financial resources for school arts programs as well as hints for contacting resources and dealing with sponsors.

Number 7 - *The Case for the Arts in School*
Presents a rationale for arts in education.

Number 8 - *Arts in the Curriculum*
Provides suggestions for integrating the arts into the regular school curriculum.

Number 9 - *Creative Collaborations: Artists, Teachers, and Students*
Guidelines for forming partnerships between artists and people in schools.

Number 10 - *Arts in the Classroom: What One Elementary Teacher Can Do*
Describes different ways that elementary school teachers can bring arts into the classroom.

The Arts, Education, and Americans Panel. *Coming to Our Senses: The Significance of the Arts for American Education*. New York: McGraw-Hill, 1977. The classic comprehensive report on arts and education.

Board of Education of the City of New York. *Arts in General Education: An Administrator's Manual*. New York, 1979.
(Available from the Board of Education of the City of New York, Publications Sales Office, 110 Livingston Street, Brooklyn, New York 11201.)
"This manual is designed to help elementary and secondary school administrators create an Arts in General Education (AGE) Program consistent with the needs of their school community. It offers guidelines for organizational planning, staff and curriculum development, as well as specific processes and suggestions for interdisciplinary arts projects related to the AGE program." - Preface

Brittain, W. Lambert. *Creativity, Art, and the Young Child*. New York: Macmillan, 1979.
Offers research findings on the art of young children.

California State Department of Education. *Promising Programs in Arts Education*, 1976. Sacramento: California State Department of Education, P.O. Box 271, 95802.
Brief descriptions of different types of exemplary arts programs: multi-arts experiences, in-school programs that focus on one discipline, and school-community programs.

Chapman, Laura H., *Instant Art, Instant Culture: the Unspoken Policy for American Schools*. New York: Teachers College Press, 1982.
Presents a thoughtful critique of arts-in-education programs and policies and proposes alternative approaches.

Eddy, Junius. *Seattle's Arts for Learning Project: An Evaluative Report*. Seattle Public Schools, Seattle, Washington, 1978.
The author evaluates Seattle's arts program on the basis of observations and conversations with school staff, students, parents, and community arts organizations.

Eisner, Elliot W., ed. *The Arts, Human Development, and Education*. Berkeley, Calif.: McCutchan, 1976.
Deals with theories of children's artistic development as well as with the practical aspects of developing school arts programs.

Environmental Education Program of the American Institute of Architects. *The Sourcebook: Learning by Design*, 1981. American Institute of Architects, 1735 New York Avenue N.W., Washington, D.C. 20006.
A catalogue of teaching resources related to both the built and natural environments.

Federal Council on the Arts and Humanities. *Cultural Directory 2: Federal Funds and Services for the Arts and Humanities.* Washington, D.C.: Smithsonian Institution Press, 1980.
Describes federal programs that provide funds and services for the arts and humanities.

The Foundation Center. *The Foundation Directory.* Edition 8, 1981. The Foundation Center, 888 Seventh Avenue, New York, New York 10019.
Provides information about nongovernmental grantmaking foundations in the United States and the primary interests of each of these foundations.

Fowler, Charles B., ed. *An Arts in Education Source Book: A View from the JDR 3rd Fund.* The JDR 3rd Fund, New York, 1980.
Presents case studies of arts-in-education programs and suggests strategies for integrating the arts into the general curriculum.

Gardner, Howard. *The Arts and Human Development.* New York: John Wiley & Sons, 1973.
Relates findings in developmental psychology to the artistic process.

Goldberg, Lillian. *The Touchstone Study.* Forthcoming, 1983. Touchstone Center, 141 East 88th Street, New York 10028.
The author evaluates the Center's "thematic" process, over a period of a year, relating it to imaginitive and creative concerns of children and teachers. The approach to evaluation provides an interesting model for other arts-in-education programs.

Hausman, Jerome J., ed. *Arts and the Schools.* New York: McGraw-Hill, 1980.
Provides a rationale for arts programs in schools, an analysis of children's developmental stages, and a discussion of program implementation. An extensive annotated bibliography is also included.

Introduction to Grantsmanship. A collection of reprints from *The Grantmanship Center News,* published bi-monthly by the Grantsmanship Center, 1021 South Grand Avenue, Los Angeles, California, 90015.
The collection contains such information as how to identify potential funding sources, ideas for public relations for nonprofit organizations, and suggestions for program planning and proposal writing.

Jenness, Aylette. *Creating a Partnership: Museums and Schools,* 1980. Cultural Education Collaborative, 164 Newbury Street, Boston, Massachusetts 02116.
Describes the step-by-step process four schools went through in order to create an ongoing alliance with a museum.

Lincoln Center Institute Report. Lincoln Center for the Performing Arts, 140 West 65th Street, New York, New York 10023.
Reports of Lincoln's Center Institute, a program that provides arts training for elementary and secondary school teachers.

Madeja, Stanley S., and Onuska, Sheila. *Through the Arts to the Aesthetic.* St. Louis: CEMREL, 1977.
Describes an elementary school curriculum for aesthetic education developed by CEMREL, Inc.

_____ et al. *Final Report on the Institute in Aesthetic Education for Administrators,* Volume 1, *An 8 Day Week.* St. Louis: CEMREL, 1974.
A report on an institute designed to show administrators how aesthetic programs can be implemented.

Minnesota Alliance for Arts in Education. *All the Arts for All the Kids: An Advocacy Handbook for Arts Education Programs.* MAAE, Post Office Box 13039, Minneapolis, Minnesota 55414.
Practical suggestions for planning, funding, maintaining, and evaluating school arts programs.

The National Elementary Principal, 55 (January / February 1976).
The articles in this issue, "The Ecology of Education: The Arts," include Stanley S. Madeja, "The Arts in the Curriculum"; John Hoare Kerr, "Artists in Educational Settings: A Report from the National Endowment for the Arts"; Robert E. Stake and Gordon A. Hoke, "Evaluating an Arts Program: Movement and Dance in a Downstate District"; Jack W. Kukuk and James A. Sjolund, "Arts for the Handicapped: A National Direction"; and others.

Newsom, Barbara Y., and Silver, Adele Z., *The Art Museum as Educator: A Collection of Studies as Guides to Practice and Policy.* Berkeley: University of California Press, 1977.
Gives case studies of more than one hundred museum educational programs throughout the country.

Office of the National Coordinator of Visual Arts and Crafts for the National Endowment for the Arts: *Visual Artists and Craftsmen in Schools,* 1979. National Endowment for the Arts, 2401 East State Street, N.W., Washington, D.C. 20506.
Provides artists, schools, and agencies with basic information for use in designing arts programs.

Oklahoma State Department of Education. *A New Wind Blowing: Arts in Education in Oklahoma Schools.* Oklahoma State Department of Education, Room 332, Oliver Hodge Building, 2500 North Lincoln, Oklahoma City, Oklahoma 73105.
Describes Oklahoma's arts-in-education programs and what makes them work.

Pierce, Catherine. *Troubled Youth and the Arts: A Resource Guide*. Silver Springs, Maryland: Read, Inc., 1979.

Porter, Robert, A., ed. *Arts Advocacy: A Citizen Action Manual*, 1980. American Council for the Arts, 570 Seventh Avenue, New York, New York 10018.
"A mix of commentary, practical tips on how to develop a campaign, and case descriptions of selected advocacy programs throughout the country." - Introduction.

_____. *Guide to Corporate Giving 3*, 1983. American Council for the Arts, 570 Seventh Avenue, New York, New York 10018.
Identifies arts contributions policies of certain corporations and their areas of interest.

Principal 60 (September 1980).
The articles in this issue, "The Uncertain World of Arts Education," include Martin Engel, "Getting Serious about Arts Education"; Elliot Eisner, "The Arts as a Way of Knowing"; Thomas Hatfield, "Things You Need to Know About Developing an Arts Program"; Sidney Trubowitz and Richard Lewis, "Art Made Me Somebody: The Importance of Arts for the Handicapped"; and others.

Remer, Jane. *Changing Schools Through the Arts*. New York: McGraw-Hill, 1982.
Addresses the role of the arts in schools and provides strategies for getting them there.

Shapiro, Stephen R.; Place, Richard; and Scheidenhelm, Richard. *Artists in the Classroom*. Hartford, Conn.: Connecticut Commission on the Arts, 1973.
Presents case studies of visiting artists working in classrooms.

Shuker, Nancy, ed. *Arts in Education Partners: Schools and Their Communities*. Jointly sponsored by the Juior League of Oklahoma City, the Arts Council of Oklahoma City, Oklahoma City Public Schools, the Association of Junior Leagues, and the JDR 3rd Fund, 1977. (Available from the American Council for the Arts Publications, 570 Seventh Avenue, New York, New York 10018.)
Gives case studies of arts-in-education programs in several cities.

South Carolina Department of Education. *Comprehensive Arts Planning Guide*, 1976. South Carolina Department-of-Education, 803 Rutledge Building, Columbia, South Carolina 29201.
A step-by-step guide for planning arts-education programs. Sections also deal with specialized arts for the handicapped and for the gifted.

Stake, Robert, ed. *Evaluating the Arts in Education: A Responsive Approach.* Columbus: Charles E. Merrill, 1975.
Presents a rationale and methods of evaluating arts-in-education programs. Examples of evaluation reports and an annotated bibliography are also included.

Sterling, Carol, and Bolin, Mary Jane. *Arts Proposal Writing: A Sourcebook of Ideas for Writing Proposals for Any School Program*, 1982. Educational Improvement Center - Central 3684 U.S. Route 1, Building 1, Princeton, New Jersey 08540.
"A funding booklet which is specifically designed to take the fear out of proposal writing and to give you some skills and techniques that can help you to bring your best ideas for arts programs to a lively reality." - Foreword

_____. *Support for School Arts Programs: A Sourcebook of Ideas for Promotion of Any School Program*, 1981. Education Improvement Center - Central, 3684 U.S. Route 1, Building 1, Princeton, New Jersey 08540.
Offers ideas for sparking community support in school arts programs.

PART II: NATIONAL ORGANIZATIONS

Affiliate Artists, Inc.
155 West 68th Street
New York, New York 10023
Arranges residencies of young performing artists in schools, factories, and other settings across the country.

Alliance for Arts Education
John F. Kennedy Center for the Performing Arts
Washington, D.C. 20566
This information source for arts organizations and agencies provides technical assistance for those developing arts programs for children and young adults.

American Association of Museums
1055 Thomas Jefferson Street, N.W.
Washington, D.C. 20007
A service organization that promotes museums as cultural and educational resources and produces publications.

American Council for the Arts
570 Seventh Avenue
New York, New York 10018
Offers management training, general advocacy for the arts, and many publications.

American Craft Council
22 West 55th Street
New York, New York 10019
The resource and education department maintains a resource facility on contemporary American crafts.

American Dance Guild
570 Seventh Avenue
New York, New York 10018
Provides a resource center for dance materials, curriculum development services, publications, films, and workshops.

American Institute of Architects
1735 New York Avenue N. W.
Washington, D. C. 20006
Develops teacher-training and resource materials regarding built environments.

American Theatre Association
1010 Winconsin Avenue
Washington, D. C. 20007
Provides curriculum development, staff development consultation, drama in special education assistance, resident artist services, and publications.

The Arts, Education and Americans, Inc.
John F. Kennedy Center for the Performing Arts
Washington, D. C. 20566
Provides resources that help groups at local levels advocate for the continuation and expansion of the arts in the schools.

Education Resources Information Center (ERIC)
National Institute of Education
U.S. Department of Health, Education, and Welfare
Washington, D. C. 20208
"ERIC makes available through hundreds of libraries and information centers over 100,000 unpublished, hard-to-find documents on all phases, levels, and subject areas of education."

Educational Film Library Association
43 West 61st Street
New York, New York 10023
A national information center for 16mm films and other nonprint media for educational uses that offers reference and advisory services, publications, and a film festival.

Music Educators National Conference
1902 Association Drive
Reston, Virginia 22091
A voluntary nonprofit organization that offers publications, workshops, and seminars of interest to music educators.

National Art Education Association
1916 Association Drive
Reston, Virginia 22091
A resource and membership organization for art teachers that distributes publications concerning arts education.

National Committee - Arts for the Handicapped
1825 Connecticut Avenue N.W., Suite 418
Washington, D.C. 20009
Supports research activities and disseminates information on the arts and the handicapped.

National Endowment for the Arts
Artists-in-Education Program
Washington, D.C. 20506
Involved in the placement of artists in elementary and secondary schools.

Teachers and Writers Collaborative
84 Fifth Avenue
New York, New York 10011
Brings writers and other artists in contact with teachers and students and distributes publications.

Young Audiences, Inc.
115 East 92nd Street
New York, New York 10028
Brings performing arts programs to schools such as performances, workshops, residencies, and technical assistance for teachers. Works through their local chapters. Publishes handbooks from time to time.

Index

Design: The Laughing Bear Associates
Photography Preparation: AfterImage
Printing: Northlight Studio Press